UNCLE SWAMI

Also by Vijay Prashad

The Darker Nations:
A People's History of the Third World

Keeping Up with the Dow Joneses:
Stocks, Jails, Welfare

Everybody Was Kung Fu Fighting:
Afro-Asian Connections and the Myth of Cultural Purity

Fat Cats and Running Dogs:
The Enron Stage of Capitalism

War Against the Planet:
The Fifth Afghan War, Imperialism, and
Other Assorted Fundamentalisms

Untouchable Freedom:
A Social History of a Dalit Community

The Karma of Brown Folk

UNCLE SWAMI

SOUTH ASIANS IN AMERICA TODAY

Vijay Prashad

Requests for permission to reproduce selections
from this book should be mailed to:
Permissions Department, The New Press, 38 Greene Street,
New York, NY 10013.

Published in the United States by The New Press, New York, 2012
Distributed by Perseus Distribution

LIBRARY OF CONGRESS CATALOGING-IN-PUBLICATION DATA

Prashad, Vijay.
Uncle Swami: South Asians in America Today / Vijay Prashad.
        p.   cm.
Includes index.
ISBN 978-1-59558-784-8 (hc. : alk. paper)
1. South Asian Americans—Social conditions.   2. South Asian
Americans—Ethnic identity.   3. South Asian Americans—Cultural
assimilation.   4. September 11 Terrorist Attacks, 2001—Influence.   5. United
States—Race relations—21st century   I. Title.
E184.S69P74 2012
305.895'073—dc23   2011037344

The New Press was established in 1990 as a not-for-profit alternative to the
large, commercial publishing houses currently dominating the book publishing
industry. The New Press operates in the public interest rather than for private
gain, and is committed to publishing, in innovative ways, works of educational,
cultural, and community value that are often deemed insufficiently profitable.

www.thenewpress.com

Composition by dix!
This book was set in Electra

Printed in the United States of America

2   4   6   8   10   9   7   5   3   1

For Ishan Bose-Pyne (1994–2010)

Jazz musician, chess maestro, physics whiz, radical visionary.
Always "looking for that great jazz note
to destroy the walls of Jericho."

CONTENTS

PREFACE

I still think today as yesterday that the color line is a great problem of this century. But today I see more clearly than yesterday that back of the problem of race and color, lies a greater problem which both obscures and implements it: and that is the fact that so many civilized persons are willing to live in comfort even if the price of this is poverty, ignorance, and disease of the majority of their fellowmen; that to maintain this privilege men have waged war until today war tends to become universal and continuous, and the excuse for this war continues largely to be color and race.

—W.E.B. Du Bois, 1953 Preface to *The Souls of Black Folk*

This book is about the South Asian American community after 9/11, and so in many aspects is about the ways in which many of us took cover behind liberal tolerance to get to the other side of the most difficult period of the domestic impact of the War on Terror. People of South Asian ancestry, so easily mistaken as terrorists, have by now come to terms with the reality of racism and of profiling. Few *desis* (a person of Indian, Pakistani, Bangladeshi, Afghani, Sri Lankan, or Nepalese descent) are able to deny the existence of a heightened fear of our bodies after 9/11 and after the ramped-up machinery of fear that came from the Bush administration, the feverish 24/7 media attention, and the general air of suspicion that descended upon our fellow residents of this territory. But what many of us do not accept is the intimate relationship between this very racism that we acknowledge and the imperial ambitions of the United States. *Uncle Swami*, this extended essay of mine written to update the formulations in my *Karma of Brown Folk*, hopes to make the case for this intimate relationship—to show not only that the excuse for war continues largely to be color and race, but that war making is a natural outgrowth of the culture of hierarchy within the United States, a culture that has resulted in the creation of vast swaths of disposable people for whose control we have created an archipelago of prisons and ghettos, and a culture that relies upon spending on the military rather than on social goods to maintain its equilibrium.

Human freedom demands that we dismiss the politics of fear and offer a program for authentic security. Our politics—the politics of solidarity, of well-being, and of consideration—asks us to recognize that our so-called adversaries are themselves angry not for inherent or cultural reasons but because they too are survivors in the world of economic insecurity and of fear. It asks us to experiment with whatever intellectual and practical resources we have to produce a new foundation for life. Everybody dies, but not everybody lives. Everybody has to have a chance to live.

ACKNOWLEDGMENTS

Sections of this book were previously published in *Amerasia* (edited by Russell Leong), *Counterpunch* (edited by Alexander Cockburn and Jeffrey St. Clair), *Desi Rap* (edited by Ajay Nair and Murali Balaji), *Economic and Political Weekly* (edited by Srinivasan Ramani), *Frontline* (edited by R. Vijayashankar), *Global Dialogue* (edited by Paul Theodoulou), *Middle East Report* (edited by Chris Toensing), *Monthly Review* (edited by John Bellamy Foster), *Namaste Sharon* (edited by Sudhanva Deshpande), *Race/Ethnicity: Multidisciplinary Global Contexts* (edited by Deepa Iyer), *South Atlantic Quarterly* (edited by John L. Jackson), *Social Analysis* (edited by George Baca), *Student Struggle* (edited by G. Selva), and the *Asian American Literary Review* (edited by Parag Khandhar and Rajini Srikanth).

Many of the formulations were introduced and debated in talks at colleges and community events, at protests and car rides, at family gatherings and over pots of tea with friends. In alphabetical order, special thanks to Mona Ahmad Ali, Taz Ahmad, Ulka Anjaria, Zayde Antrim, Rishi Awantramani, Bill Ayers, Raymond Baker, Vivek Bald, Davarian Baldwin, Janet

Bauer, Martha Biondi, Prasenjit Bose, Shonali Bose, Janaki Challa, Rosa Clemente, Jo Comerford, Manuel Criollo, Shilpa Dave, Alfredo de Avila, Libero Della Piana, Bharavi Desai, Sudhanva Deshpande, Pawan Dhingra, Bernardine Dohrn, Rena Fraden, Craig Gilmore, Ruthie Gilmore, Kifah Hanna, Annie Harper, Andy Hsiao, Shafqat Hussain, Naeem Inayatul-lah, Deepa Iyer, Anjali Kamat, Nitasha Kaul, Robin Kelley, Sorayya Khan, Parag Khandhar, Bakari Kitwana, Surabhi Kukke, Amitava Kumar, Scott Kurashige, Tammy Bang Liu, Daniella Mahones, Rekha Malhotra, Sunaina Maira, Eric Mann, Seth Markle, Biju Mathew, Monami Maulik, Qalan-dar Bux Memon, Ali Mir, Raza Mir, Naeem Mohaiemen, Tej Nagaraj, Jeff Napolitano, Mark Anthony Neal, Prachi Patan-kar, Harish Patel, Gautam Premnath, Prabir Purkayastha, Kym Ragusa, Junaid Rana, Barbara Ransby, Kasturi Ray, Srirupa Ray, Sujani Reddy, Anamik Saha, P. Sainath, Alis Sandosharaj, Rinku Sen, Madhu Singh, Sonny Singh Brooklynwala, Saket Soni, Rajini Srikanth, Amita Swadin, Mark Toney, Alladin Ul-lah, Lalit Vachani, Linta Varghese, Manu Vimalasserry, Mau-rice Wade, Johnny Williams, and so many, many more. And then, Agha Shahid Ali (I'll meet you in Kashmir), Kartar Dhil-lon (one more cup of tea in Berkeley), Reetika Vazirani and Jehan (the bed is still made up), and Miguel Luna (one more swig of ginger brandy). My editor on this book is Marc Favreau, who saw its potential (and my production editor, Sarah Fan, whose patient efficiency helped manage my errors). My family in Calcutta, Delhi, and California are my anchor (especially my mother, Soni Prashad). My reader was Lisa Armstrong, who has the best bullshit radar for my writings. Zalia and Rosa, my cities of many lights.

1

Letter to Uncle Swami

Dear Uncle Swami,

It has been ten years since the planes crashed into your buildings. It was a shock to your system. You were not used to such things. It didn't break your heart. It sharpened your rage. Like an exhausted dragon, you whipped your tail around, crashing into other buildings, these in far-off Kabul and Kandahar, Mazar-e-Sharif and Herat, later Baghdad and Basra, and your feet stomped on your own ground, crushing Balbir Singh Sodhi and Gurcharanjeet Singh Anand, Imran Tahir and Ahmed Abualeinen. These latter are just names, sitting patiently in your computer systems, either in mortuary registers or deportation files. The people behind them are shadows: you smiled at them when they served you your curries, and patted their backs when they delivered their assignments on time — but you didn't really care about them, what they were made of, their moral compasses. Planes crash, people are smashed, here and there, there and here.

Please do not take my blunt words to heart, Uncle. You have been good to me. You have been good to many of us. But, why does my stomach still clench when someone with a badge approaches me, thinking in my churned head that my time has come, I am going to be led to a plane and sent back to where I came from? Is it because that badge has started stopping me more often these past ten years, asking me why I am where I am, where I am going, what I believe in? Who are these people with badges, Uncle, and why do they stare at me?

I have heartburn, Uncle. I will take to drink. I will take to drugs. I will take to watching TV, eating fast food, going into debt. I will not exfoliate, I will not eat salad, I will not read the newspaper. I cannot wear my head scarf, I cannot grow my beard, I cannot speak my name and allow its poetry to ring through the air.

You send American aid all around, throwing money and cheese at the world's poor. Even that aid is money you have borrowed from others. Lords are thieves, whose theft is proper.

But, Uncle, there is no aid for us—all we want is your kindness, and a little decency.

Your obedient servant,
Vijay Prashad

2

The Day Our Probation Ended

... the sons of the slums cuffed up on trumped charges,
'Cause we look different, talk different, labeled as Jihadists.
—Chee Malabar, "Oblique Brown," 2006

Eleven days after 9/11, I was on the train to New York City. It was a Friday. I was teaching a class at New York University on immigration. I hadn't been into the city since before the attacks. Trying to distract myself, I read Saskia Sassen's *Guests and Aliens*. It was going to be one of the main books for our seminar. Along the way, I can't remember where, a troop of policemen came through the cabin. The train was at a station. They asked various people to follow them onto the platform. I was among them. We were asked some basic questions and then told to get back on the train.

I've seen enough World War II films to know how I should feel. There was fear, and there was anxiety. Would I, like so many others, be sent off to a deportation detention center? News reports of such removals had begun to sneak around, like a fetid rumor, among South Asians and Muslims. A Sikh man had already been killed in Arizona. Mistaken identity was the order of the day. My conversation with the officer was brief; he asked me what I was reading. It seemed that even a nonconformist book, in English, was sufficient to prove my academic credentials. No disrespect to Sassen, but a dog-eared and marked-up copy of her book would hardly be in the hands of a terrorist!

But for others, that was wishful thinking. On October 29, Tariq Ali was detained at Munich's airport—the offending article a slim volume in German of Karl Marx's *On Suicide*. Tariq had the mayor of Munich vouch for him, and he was then released. As he wrote that day, "It was a tiny enough scratch, but if untreated these can sometimes lead to gangrene."

Within minutes after the World Trade Center was hit, angry white men yelled obscenities and chased Amrik Singh Chawla of Brooklyn, New York, who had escaped from the towers, down the street. His only escape was to hide his turban in his briefcase; they had gone after him because of his turban. In Richmond, Queens, three white youth severely beat up a Sikh man; other men shot at two Sikh boys; and a white man began to yell at a Sikh man on the Northern State Parkway, "You fucking Arab rag-head, you're all going to die, we're going to kill every one of you," as all four of those in his car gave the Sikh man the finger. Men got the brunt of these attacks, because men mainly wear turbans. Those turbans served to distinguish the "evildoers." The government had not yet said anything about Osama bin Laden, who wears a turban, and yet ordinary Americans knew that the turban somehow signified the soldiers of terror. For this reason, Sikhs suffered the brunt of the early attacks after 9/11.

On September 14, outside a Manhattan meeting organized

by the South Asian Journalists Association to discuss the hate crimes, a man who was taking his baby for a walk assaulted one of the Sikh participants. "You Islamic mosquitoes should be killed," he yelled, a phrase captured by TV Asia. Manga Singh, a Sikh taxi driver, reported to the New York Taxi Workers Alliance that a passenger started to beat him with an umbrella while yelling, "I hate you. I hate you and your turban." Mr. Singh's father, Surinder Singh, is also a taxi driver, and he reported that a rider said to him, "You did that, you attacked the World Trade Center." A white man assaulted an elderly Sikh man who was then taken to the hospital, just as unknown assailants firebombed a Sikh gurudwara near Cleveland, Ohio. Balbir Singh Sodhi, a worker at an all-night store, was shot to death in Mesa, Arizona, by a man who later told the police, "I stand for America all the way."

Hours after Mr. Sodhi was found dead, an unknown assailant shot Waqar Hassan of Dallas, Texas. Mr. Hassan was at work as a store clerk at Mom's Grocery when he was shot. Mosques were included with gurudwaras in the saturnalia of random violence, just as South and West Asians of all faiths became, along with Sikhs, targets of retaliation for 9/11. The bulk of the attacks took place against not only those who are of West and South Asian descent, but against small merchants and workers, those who work the lonely, long-hour jobs at kiosks or in taxis, and those who live in minority neighborhoods.

Many professionals do not identify with victims of hate crimes because they are so infrequently affected. They are most often inconvenienced by xenophobia, opting to exaggerate their newly minted American accents or adopting nicknames in quotes (Pradip "Max" Kothari) to avoid the awkwardness of parochial peoples' hesitancy before their alien names. The events of 9/11 were a wake-up call. Mr. Ashraf Khan is a cell phone magnate. He was removed from a first-class seat on a Delta Airlines aircraft because the pilot felt that he endangered the other passengers. "I had a first-class ticket," Mr. Khan told National Public Radio, as if this should have secured him against the post-9/11 panic. South Asian film stars (Kamal Hassan and Aamir Khan), businessmen (Vijay Mallya), and writers (Rohinton Mistry and Ahmed Rashid) had to leave aircraft. The fear set in among all classes, even as the working class bore the brunt of the retaliatory violence. The volume of the attacks was not enormous, and yet a general sense of fear pervaded South and West Asians in the United States. Many refused to leave their homes to go to work or to school, and many foreign students got on the first available plane back to their homelands.

Women faced hostility in different spaces, generally not as routine assaults by those emboldened to be vigilantes for 9/11. But there are also women who faced the crowd: Meera Kumar, on September 12, 2001, was removed from an Amtrak train in Boston; in Huntington, New York, an elderly drunk driver tried to run down a Pakistani woman, followed her into a store, and threatened to kill her because she was "destroying my country"; in Los Angeles, on September 13, 2001, an Iranian woman was punched in the eye by another woman who wanted to register her displeasure with those who look like terrorists; on September 15, 2001, when Kimberly Lowe, a Creek Native American, stopped her car in Tulsa, Oklahoma, to confront a group of white males who had yelled, "Go back to your own country," they pinned her down and drove over her till she died.

She was mistaken for the wrong kind of Indian.

The turban has always provoked anxiety; the Sikhs who came to California in the nineteenth century were greeted with hostility. But the Sikhs didn't take it lightly: "I used to go to Maryville every Saturday," one man recounted in the 1920s. "One day a drunk *ghora* [white man] came out of a bar and motioned to me saying, 'Come here, slave!' I said I was no slave man. He told me that his race ruled India and America, too. All we were slaves. He came close to me and I hit him and got away fast." There was no such self-defense after 9/11. The U.S. media began to run stories of ordinary Muslims testifying against the 9/11 attacks. They stood before television cameras and condemned the terrorists. Their body language quivered. Anthropologist Jessica Falcone remarked how, after 9/11, the Sikh community in the Washington, D.C., area bent over backward to prove its patriotism. A *Washington Post* journalist visited a Sikh community leader, who told her, "We condemn harassment, we condemn terrorism. We are American, and we fully support the Bush administration." One of his nephews had just been shot at because of his turban. "We are united as Sikhs," he told the reporter, "and as Americans." Meanwhile, up in New York City's Washington Heights, I saw white men with small U.S. flags make the rounds of the immigrant-owned small grocery stores. They banged these flags, which retailed at about $1 each, on counters and said things like "Aren't you going to be a patriot and buy this flag?" The flags cost the immigrant workers $5 each, but they were far too scared to refuse. The test of loyalty provided a business opportunity for the young white men, and it forced the small shops to fly as many flags as possible. Patriotism is not, in this instance, the refuge of scoundrels. It is an act of desperation.

In a comprehensive review of over a thousand hate attacks on Arabs and desis, Human Rights Watch noted, "This violence was directed at people solely because they shared or were perceived as sharing the national background or religion of the hijackers and al-Qaeda members deemed responsible for attacking the World Trade Center and the Pentagon." The report is well titled *"We Are Not the Enemy": Hate Crimes Against Arabs, Muslims, and Those Perceived to Be Arab or Muslim After September 11*. A report from the South Asian American Leaders for Tomorrow found that in the week after 9/11, the U.S. media reported 645 bias incidents directed toward Americans perceived to be of Middle Eastern descent. The irony in all this was that among the hijackers none were from South Asia. They were Saudis and Egyptians, and seemed to have spent most of their time in Europe, with only a brief detour in Afghanistan. Anthropological and geopolitical distinctions seemed to make no difference. It was sufficient if you resembled a terrorist: olive skin, turbans, head scarves, facial hair, and other such tokens were the markers of danger. It is why Sikh men came into the dragnet early; Osama bin Laden also wore a turban. None of the hijackers wore a turban, or had other outward signs of religiosity. A terrorist does not announce himself or herself. That would defeat the purpose. But the visual sign is precisely what the racist would like to focus on, exactly what the terrorist would like to deny. The bodies of so many are stripped bare by this contradiction.

TWICE-BORN GENERATION

My brother moved to California in the 1980s, and I followed along in his train. He worked in San Leandro, a town devoted to the maintenance of cars and car culture. On the weekend, the Indian American community would gather in each other's homes. The people in the room were warm and friendly to each other, with the men in one room, the women in another, and the children in the basement or the den, with their "home" friends. I was too old to be with the kids, most of whom were born in the United States, and too young to mingle with the adults. That curious age allows one to wander between sets.

I remain enthralled by two facts about these adults:

1. They were also highly educated men and women, who held various kinds of professional jobs in their new country. Not more than a decade in their new land, they had already attained positions of prominence in their fields — not as leaders, to be sure, but as accomplished technicians (as doctors, engineers, scientists, and even in the less sure world of midrange business).

2. They had almost no interest in politics or in the issues of the day. No one much liked Reagan, but that seemed largely a temperamental thing — his casualness seemed inappropriate for a world leader. If the discussion turned to politics, it was most often about India, and here too the trend seemed staged: either nostalgia for the kind of political talk of their college days, or animosity for this or that policy of the government (the textbook was *India*

West and *India Abroad*, the newspapers of record for the
Indian American community).

Occasionally there was a bit of guilt about leaving India behind, to be part of the brain drain; this led to the very rare bout
of collective charity (to raise money for this or that orphanage,
or school of the blind, or earthquake relief—all based in India).
Nearby Oakland burned with the futility of the modern world,
but it would only come into our conversation if talk turned to
the vegetables to be found at its Chinatown.

Nothing of this should be a surprise. The middle class seeks
convenience, and is loath to turn to politics when it might
inconvenience one's daily life or one's sense of moral equilibrium. That's a universally enforced silence. Nor should it
come as a surprise that the migrants who have come into the
United States after 1965 have no well-developed social obligation to the struggles that enabled them to have such success.
The road to Indian America was paved by the toil of others,
now barely acknowledged. Born in the 1940s and 1950s, this
generation of middle-class Indians missed the freedom struggle. Some of them would have had parents or grandparents in
the fight, but they did not lift the cudgels for their homeland.
When they went to school and college, now funded by the
hard labor of their co-citizens in the new nation, they did not
feel the weight of subordination and exclusion. It was a privilege to breathe the air of freedom, and to feel a part of a new
dawn. That is the first birth of those who would become Indian
Americans.

Their second birth is equal to the first. The United States
barred Indians from entry into the country between 1924 and

1965. The law changed in 1965 as a result of the United States' fear that the USSR might overtake it in the science, technology, and arms race (the Soviet-launched satellite, Sputnik, in 1957 sent fear into the spinal cord of the nation). The new immigration law allowed migrants to enter if they brought with them special technical and scientific skills, as well as medical degrees (to help staff the expanded Medicare system, also in operation from the mid-1960s). This was the reason I was surrounded by doctors and engineers on those Friday nights. But the story is not complete yet. The immigration act also came alongside two landmark laws, the Civil Rights Act (1964) and the Voting Rights Act (1965). At least two generations of people sacrificed their lives and longings to overturn the injustice of Jim Crow. Because of them, the new migrants who entered the universities and laboratories, hospitals and research centers could live with the formal promise of equality. Once more the air of freedom, and of a new beginning.

Indian Americans did not know political struggles for freedom. In India they were born after independence had been won, and in the United States they arrived after the civil rights battles had already won them dignity and rights. This doubly privileged population also had the incredible fortune of state-supported education and state-selected immigration practices to give them the feeling that they were invincible—the massive social network that delivered them their advantages was invisible to them. Their blindness to their twice-born status was helped along by the U.S. establishment media that championed them as a "model minority" (one that did not need welfare and overt state support), and by the Indian establishment, which, by the 1980s, celebrated their overseas success and longed for their surplus investments—"better brain drain," Prime Minister Rajiv Gandhi said, "than brain in the drain."

Such a narrow political vision ill-prepared Indian Americans for the events after 9/11. Floundering with the polite accommodations so typical of middle-class migrants, the Indian Americans had nothing in their arsenal to push back against the sudden cataclysm. Oscillation between outrage and cowering was the main frequency for their reaction.

RACE AND THE BIRTH OF THE SOUTH ASIAN AMERICAN

At those weekend parties, I would eat with the children. My task was to make sure that they did not spill their drinks on the sofas and that they ate without too much complaint. It was not an unpleasant task. They had much to offer in entertainment, naughty in the way of migrant children thrown together, some related and some not, feeling comfortable in their skin among children who had similar parents and similar schoolmates— two worlds that otherwise wouldn't know each other, but familiar to all of them. Of course, I was eager to be elsewhere, too old for this but with neither the cash nor the car to cry havoc in the world of my peers.

Years later, as a community organizer in Providence, Rhode Island, I met the contemporaries of these children, now college students in their own right. I was running a campaign for Direct Action for Rights and Equality (DARE) against tobacco advertisements in the neighborhoods mainly populated by African Americans, Dominican Americans, and Hmong Americans. We got a spot on our local television channel. The next morning I got a phone call from a student at Brown University. Pooja Sarin was a representative of the South Asian Students' Association (SASA), and they wanted to see about doing some community service. A few days later, the SASA executive board ("exec board") came to see me on Lockwood Avenue. They were nervous about being in this part of town but eager to be involved. Everything about them moved me: the memories of the childhood of young adults like them in far-off California, and the reality that they wanted to devote some of their energy to matters far removed from their own lives.

Born in largely white suburbs, these young people also gathered on weekends to meet the children of immigrants like their parents. But they had been otherwise isolated from their parents' homelands; the occasional summer trips did not fully mark their lives. They came of age on the wave of multiculturalism, which in the affluent and modest suburbs meant a great deal of tolerance for the educated migrant. It would all change a generation later, when the migrants into the suburbs and ex-urbs were working-class Latinos. It was already difficult when the entrant was African or African American. The hierarchies of racial acceptance cushioned the Indians and their families (there are always the anecdotes of humiliation, but these were not central). When these young people went to college in the 1990s, a new form of racial belonging emerged. They became "South Asian American," a term that does not refer to a place (South Asia) but to a sense of community among children of parents from the various countries of South Asia. These parents might not have that much in common (Sri Lankans would not meet socially with Pakistanis), but their children saw the connections intuitively. The content of their cultural lives might have been different, but the *form* was the same: South Asian parents, with their own robust connections to their homelands and their own ideas about raising children, and American schools and friends, with their own worldviews and expectations. It was this duality that was shared across these students. Scholar Sunaina Maira, in *Desis in the House*, cleverly called this process "reverse assimilation."

The cultural links were the subjective connection. The objective basis for the emergence of the South Asian American was the nature of social life on college campuses. College multiculturalism operated on the basis of a binary: there are the "normal" students whose social life is already well provided for, and those "other" students who come from previously invisible populations—African Americans, Latinos, Asian Americans, women, lesbians and gays, and international students. To bring them to life, the colleges and universities provided funds for organizations and events. It is in this space that the children of the Indian migrants found, and continue to find, their association with children of migrants from Pakistan, Sri Lanka, Bangladesh, and Nepal. There was often a minor struggle to gain a foothold in the Asian American organization, but that was not serious; most students created the equivalent of SASA. By 1989, the most energetic SASA organizations joined together to create an annual SASA conference, typically held in January.

I first went to a SASA conference in 1996. Among the organizers were those who had come to seek me out three years before. We had worked together on various projects, and they had been to some protests in downtown Providence. It was an education for all of us. For the conference in 1996, SASA invited Urvashi Vaid, a leading voice in the gay and lesbian movement, as the keynote speaker. It was a singular choice, and unlikely that their parents would have chosen Urvashi to keynote one of the community events; the political gulf between the parents and children could not have been any wider. Urvashi spoke for the heart of the progressive traditions in the subcontinent and in the diaspora. She invoked Gandhi to put morality at the center of our politics, not just power:

> Gandhi wrote that morality consists of doing what we ought to do. He argued that mere observance of custom and usage was not morality. That moral actions are those guided by justice and respect for the divine will. That moral acts involve no coercion and are not motivated by self-interest. If I help my neighbor because he is suffering, I commit a moral act. If I help my neighbor because I want credit for helping him through his suffering, my action may still be a good deed, but in Gandhi's argument is not moral. Merely by pursuing our own liberation and freedom we are not engaged in a moral course. If we place our liberation movement in the service of building a more just society then we will be a movement that is unstoppable because our course will be spiritually and politically just.

Urvashi's charge is profound, and essential. It was not enough to think of advancement in terms of ethnicity. One had to have a more capacious sense of the future. The contradictions of social life on American campuses and the contradictions of American society had clarified many things for the South Asian Americans. The panels at the SASA conference covered such themes as racism, sexism, homophobia, the role of religion, the place of the university, and so on. At one level, this could have been a Black Students' Conference, or a Latino/a Students' Conference—the themes covered were the same, if the analysis and the context were different.

Certainly, one should not be too rosy-eyed in this narrative. Many of those who worked in SASA or around it found ethnicity to be a viable platform for social mobility. SASA morphed for the graduates into the Network of South Asian Professionals. The bulk of that generation, like their educated peers, went into the world of finance and technology, armed with the advantages of multiculturalism. Notable examples include Jawed Karim of YouTube, Ashwin Navin of BitTorrent, and Sandeep Chatterjee of SourceTrace. That these are all men is notable, and is the reason attorney Harshini Ali created the Network for South Asian American Women Entrepreneurs and Professionals in 2010. Migrants from India set the stage for the South Asian Americans with the creation of such platforms as The Indus Entrepreneurs (TiE) in Silicon Valley in 1992. Gurus such as Kanwal Rekhi (Excelan), Kiran Mazumdar-Shaw (Biocon), Vinod Khosla (Khosla Ventures), and Rajat Gupta (McKinsey & Company) tended to their younger *shishyas* (disciples) at regular meetings. TiE took its mentorship model across the United States and then to India (it now boasts a membership of thirteen thousand). The professional worlds of law, business, and technological development are suffused with South Asian Americans, driven to the high-octane pressure of these environments by their overachieving parents, by the advantages of multiculturalism, and by the economic boom for the privileged that escalated in the 1990s. They went into the mainstream fortified by a diet that included an understanding of how race operates in America, inculcated in college more by their own practical experiences than by the classes they took. Nothing would convince them to turn their eyes critically to U.S. imperial adventures or to the unhappy consciousness of American urban decay. But yet, there is an awareness of the operations of race, an awareness much more articulated in the world of their peers who went into the nonprofit sector.

By the 1990s, as these young people left college, it was hard to walk into a nonprofit organization anywhere in the United States and not find a South Asian American on the staff; it was equally difficult to find a civil rights legal office without a South Asian American. Well-educated lawyers cut their teeth in the Asian American Legal Defense Fund (Parag Khandhar, Chaumtoli Huq, Tito Sinha) or in the NAACP's legal department (Vanita Gupta), while other professionally trained people would become tenant organizers and advocates for the poor, builders of women's shelters, and reporters for the submerged truths of everyday life. Some of them would form South Asians for Justice in 2011, building on the work of SAALT (South Asian American Leaders of Tomorrow, formed in 2000), led by Deepa Iyer, another lawyer who moved swiftly to the better side of history. Taking the best of their advantages, and unlike many of their parents, they threw themselves into a wider political world. After all, unlike their parents, they *were* American, and not always immigrants; and, again unlike their parents, they had lived the contradictions of coming of age in the United States. For them, their privileges do not come as if by chance. They recognize their own history.

But the negotiation of the gap between the maintenance of

one's culture in the context of xenophobia and the need to challenge elements of that cultural formation was not the privilege of those born and raised in the United States. Others had experiences that forced them to both defend their heritage and to challenge its offensive elements. To do this complex job, many had taken refuge in the term South Asian American to signal their distance from the narrowness of their national cultures. Politically and socially active members of the earlier generation had independently generated the South Asian American platform. For example, by the mid-1980s, South Asian women from New Jersey to the Bay Area formed organizations to take charge of an unmentioned violence against women and children. From Manavi in New Jersey to Narika in San Francisco, these organizations did not wish to associate themselves with the mainstream cultures of the subcontinent that promoted patriarchy as routine. To push against the cruel cultural nationalism, these groups had, separately from the college associations, begun to use the term "South Asian American." It was a term that would be adopted by South Asian American gay and lesbian organizations, as well as by other culturally and politically progressive groups that took a "panethnic approach." ("Panethnic groups," scholar Yen Le Espiritu wrote in 1994, "are products of political and social processes, rather than cultural bonds." These often emerge, she argues, "to contest systems of racism and inequality in American society"; in this case, they emerge to contest systems of patriarchy and homophobia within the cultural worlds of the migrants.) The pathway to South Asian America for the young college graduates in the 1990s was paved by these pioneers, who set up space in the activist and nonprofit world for struggle in general, and now struggle as South Asian Americans.

In these new South Asian American organizations, there was less anxiety about upward mobility and assimilation. The general ideology that governed them recognized how race operated in the United States, and it had a faint inkling of the role of imperialism and militarism in the foundation of the U.S. polity. This ideology was an invaluable resource after 9/11, and it provided the courage among some of the South Asian American groups to openly confront both the outrages of racism and the horizon of wars that emerged from Washington.

JACKSON HEIGHTS DAYS

Migration is never the simple act of transplantation. To come to the United States from Asia requires some resources. The very poor cannot move, unless they are trapped in the networks of international sex or drug trafficking. Those who have some means but recognize that their fortune will not be made in their homelands seek to mortgage what they have for distant, more promising places. When they move from places like India or Pakistan to Europe or the United States, they leave places where it does not take an enormous amount of their resources to subsist in the lower middle or middle class: advantages of family networks in the old land allow them to pool their savings with their relatives and make modest but decent lives. When their horizons expand beyond what they have, or when political claims on them make life untenable, the journey to the other side begins. Uprooted, these migrants do not carry with them the PhDs or the MDs. Their families underwrite their journey, put talismans of good fortune in their hands, and hope that they will some day return to take others with them through the looking glass.

If they are lucky, they are able to identify a relative who has already made it to Europe or the United States; this relative then sponsors them to come over, or at the very least provides them with the cultural know-how to shape-shift from visitor to permanent resident. The arcane grammar of immigration laws is well known to the veteran, who shares with other migrants this unique talent, and who shares with them a compass of suffering and a worldview, *immigritude.*

All immigrants are united by fear.

The documented endure the humiliation of endless forms, with prying and unfriendly questions, and an array of acronyms to slot us into this category or that. Passports and other papers worn by clammy hands as they wait in endless queues that lead to the same airless exchange with immigration officials whose seats are cleverly placed to make them look down on us. And then the photograph: at the local photographer, dressed up even though everyone knows that the polished shoes don't make it into the frame, hair hastily brushed back with the application of a bit of spittle, the smile which is held cautiously but which becomes disjointed when the flash goes off. Then, visa in hand, more long lines in wait for the documents to be scrutinized with bored doubt, for their authenticity to be rewarded with a brusque stamp. Finally, entry into the cities of the United States or Europe, but only to persist with that fear that there has been some error, that sometime, if not now, they will come and put you on a plane that takes you away from this place.

But those who have no documents or who lack more well-heeled documentation (such as evidence of higher degrees or land ownership in the old country) are even less confident. They greet their fixer through the curtain of illegality or semi-legality. This fixer makes everything seem easy and yet does nothing to unsettle one's dread. Looming ahead are: trips to relatives in search of cash, debts called in, favors demanded; bundles of money taken to the fixer who sets up a time for departure and a payment structure once a job is fixed at the other end; darkness, either of the night of the crossing along the Rio Grande or the endless night of the containers aboard cargo ships; a tired border guard or customs official who turns and looks away when the coyote says that it is safe, or when one of your container mates has to retch, loudly; silence, frozen like a deer before a fox, hoping; finally, entry into the cities and fields of the United States or Europe, but only to persist with that fear that one's luck will soon run dry, that sometime, if not now, they will come and put you on a plane that takes you away from this place.

By the 1980s—from the waiting rooms of JFK airport, the Merchant Marine docks of New Bedford, or the borderlands of Mexico—a new breed of South Asian joined their mightier brethren. No more the highly skilled technocrats, these mi-grants worked endless shifts in small grocery stores or in motels, at gas stations or as domestic workers, as taxi drivers or on small farms. These migrants, who fanned out across the continents on both sides of the Atlantic world, huddled in family networks and created new networks through mosques, temples, and gurudwaras. Young Pakistani men in Italy working at carnivals longed to move to Brooklyn as older Gujarati women in Iowa working in motels longed for their day to end. Dreams of other days filled long lives of toil.

People like me, professionals, interact with the working class and lower middle class either through networks of family or community, or in the interstices of our lives, when we go to buy our necessities. A grocery store sits next to Cosmos International, the remarkable store in Hartford that is owned by a family whose roots are in Eastern Europe but whose knowledge of Indian and Arab goods is legion. After filling up my car with a variety of goods (spices to soap), I often go next door to Cosmos to buy a coffee or just chat with the elderly man at the counter. He's from Surat, he tells me, and is in his seventies. His job is just a way to pass time. I come to chat with him, to "time-pass" as well. We talk about business and money, and he regales me with tales of his fellow Suratwallas, many of whom own motels. "It's a dirty business," he says with a smile in his eyes. "All those people come with their girlfriends, they stay for one or two hours, and then pay $35." The sex business brings in the regular money. "Then they have to clean the rooms, toilets, do all this work that we never did in India." But to worship in the temple of the almighty dollar, the current avatar of Vishnu, he complains, we have to do all manner of work.

He mused about the preponderance of Gujaratis, even Suratwallas, in the motel trade. Of motels in the United States today, about half are owned by desis (who also own 37 percent of the hotels). Ramesh Surati, onetime head of the Asian American Hotel Owners Association, told the Voice of America in

August 1999 that "the Patels were farmers in India, but I think we have an intrinsic substance within our blood, which is hospitality, and that has transformed us in the United States. As the fellow Asian immigrants came to this country, they saw the success that our pioneers were having and basically followed suit, and from then on, it just spread." Of such lovely myths is reality soured. In the 1950s, oil companies bought land along freeways as a speculative bid: they wanted to be sure they owned the land at the four corners of an interchange, most of which had not been planned or announced. When the interchange was established, the gas stations went up there. The surplus land along the freeway was sold to small developers, most of whom built storage units or cheap motels. A decade or so later, as Pawan Dhingra shows in *Life Behind the Lobby*, desi families pooled their money and bought into the motel trade as others abandoned what was an overbuilt and largely insolvent industry, using family labor as a way to keep the businesses afloat. The accidents of history, not necessarily anything in the blood, opened this industry to desis: racism did not allow desis many other opportunities in small business, so these became the staple of small entrepreneurs (other such venues were gas stations themselves, small stores in cities, and so on). Of course, as historian Suchetra Mazumdar argues, "the family-owned-and-operated hotel and motel business is perhaps the most extreme example of isolation and dependence in small businesses." Women work hardest in this sector: "Often located in decrepit downtowns and catering to a transient population, these low-budget hotels and motels encompass a wide range of work: room cleaning, laundry, phone reception, counter work seven days a week, twenty-four hours a day."

Indian Americans reported the highest median household income in the 2000 U.S. Census ($51,094). But a full quarter of Indian Americans live in households with incomes below $25,000. Our community has the highest rate of inequality: with a few millionaires and a considerable number who live in the basement of U.S. society. You can't go into an urban hospital in the United States without being treated by either an Indian doctor or an Indian nurse (not to speak of the nurses from the Caribbean and doctors from Africa). Yet a fifth of Indian Americans have no health insurance, a higher percentage than the national average.

Connection among Indian Americans or Pakistani Americans, or indeed South Asian Americans, is not immediate. Divides of class are deep, and remain deep, despite the emotional affinity of people trying to adjust to new homelands. Even the cavernous gap that opened up between migrant reality and normality after 9/11 was not sufficient to bring all the migrants into one camp. In fact, it might have widened.

To be a working-class and lower-middle-class Muslim after 9/11 had a special resonance. If one were a believer and wore the marks of belief (headdress, beard) and the marks of race (olive skin), survival in the streets and towns of the United States was not self-evident. The FBI operated in the community as if they had a quota. Government informants worked aggressively among vulnerable people, pushing them to plan violent acts. Osama Eldawoody earned $100,000 to "convert" Shahawar Matin Siraj, a young and susceptible man who shied away from any violence, a story told very movingly by Amitava Kumar in A *Foreigner Carrying in the Crook of His Arm a Tiny*

Bomb. FBI agent Foria Younis, meanwhile, went among young Muslims in New York, trawling for disaffection that she converted into imputed action. As a result of her work, the U.S. government deported sixteen-year-old Tashnuba Hayder to Bangladesh. They claimed that Hayder would have been the first female suicide bomber in the United States (the evidence: a one-page doodle around the word suicide, which Hayder claimed was part of her class notes on why religions opposed taking one's own life). The government held Tashnuba in detention for seven weeks, not allowing her family to visit her or to know where she was being held. Not able to find anything directly to tie her to al-Qaeda or to being a suicide bomber, the state engineered the deportation of this sixteen-year-old based on her immigration status. The *New York Times*'s Nina Bernstein interviewed Tashnuba in Dhaka, Bangladesh, where she lives with her extended family. The young girl cried, "I feel like I'm on a different planet. It just hit me. How everything happened—it's like, 'Oh, my God.'" There are now 15,000 FBI informers. This is a repeat of the 1960s-era counterintelligence program, Cointelpro 3.0.

The FBI called people like Hayder "Pepsi Jihadists" who saw "redemption in religious violence." In fact, most had no truck with jihad at all, least of all with the rants of Osama bin Laden and the feverish plots of al-Qaeda. Distance from bin Laden did not mean an embrace of U.S. society and state policy, however. Quite the contrary, which is what confused an FBI that taught itself to think in binaries ("You are either with us or against us" was hardly the motto of George W. Bush alone; it is the standard formula of political police from the

Mukhabarat of the Arab security states to the FBI of the United States).

The reaction of Yemeni American Yasser Taher to the attacks of 9/11 was emulated in households across the United States, even though most people had not traveled to Afghanistan as Taher had. When he heard the news of the attacks, Taher closed the blinds in his Lackawanna, New York, flat, went into a panic, and told his wife, "For Muslims in this country, it is all over." The local office of the FBI had an eye on a group of Lackawanna men who had been to Afghanistan, but they had no cause to go after them. After 9/11, the rules changed. The Patriot Act gave the FBI more power of surveillance and the power to arrest someone on the suspicion that they *would* commit an illegal act. The Bush administration's aggressive move overseas (in Afghanistan and, later, Iraq) was matched domestically. The FBI looked across the country to arrest anyone who they deemed might be a security risk. Part of this was for the security of the population, but most of it was for political reasons, as Dina Temple-Raston showed in *The Jihad Next Door*. The U.S. Justice Department needed to show that the new draconian laws had indeed produced some results. The Lackawanna Six, as they came to be called, were arrested on September 9, 2002, a few days before the first anniversary of 9/11. The overreached arrests of the Lackawanna Six showed the country that the Bush administration was willing to be aggressive against anyone who dared threaten the United States. The Lackawanna Six, including Taher, went to Afghanistan in error in the 1990s and recoiled at the anti-Americanism there; nevertheless, they were targets for the political police and for social safety.

After 9/11, many Muslims in the United States took refuge in their communities and in Islam. What others saw as fearful was to Muslims the heart of a heartless world, a refuge from their neighbors' hatred, so powerful that it mixed class fears with existential fears and, of all else, fears of devils incarnate, walking the streets of cities they dare not enter. Little wonder that in the land of South Asian Muslims, fear and anger led to acknowledgment of the vexed relationship around the U.S. wars between the Hindu Kush and the Atlas Mountains and their own sense of social displacement. Over the decade since 9/11, South Asian American mosques have slowly moved away from quiet fear to outrage at what the imams quite forthrightly call Islamophobia, whether in the wars overseas or in the domestic mechanisms of the War on Terror. For them, the issues were not simply about religion but about immigration and dignity. At the closing rally for the Immigrant Workers Freedom Ride (September–October 2003), Zahid Ali Syed of Local 338 Union of Food and Commercial Workers said in Flushing, "The Bangladeshi contingent was the largest. They came in about twenty buses, followed by Pakistanis, Indians, Nepalis and Sri Lankans." The gap between anti-immigration, Islamophobia, and militarism is not very wide in these communities.

On April 9, 2011, at the first major protest of the new anti-war formation United National Antiwar Committee (UNAC), three main constituents gathered and marched in New York City: socialists of various hues, peace activists, and members of the mosques of the 100 New York Imams. Muslim men, women, and children filled the ranks of the demonstration. They had come out to support the call from the 100 Imams, which was released on March 31, in the aftermath of the ridiculous hearings called by Representative Peter King on the dangers of the Muslim community in the United States. The call from the Imams states:

> We, 100 Imams from the Muslim community in New York, New Jersey, and Connecticut, stand together to thank our neighbors who have defended the Muslim community against Islamophobia. Our neighbors have stood in opposition to Congressman Peter King's hearings and against the efforts of the extremists to criminalize the practice of Islam in America.
>
> We call upon all Muslims to come out with their families on Saturday, April 9, 2011, noon at Union Square in NYC to stand in solidarity with our neighbors for justice at home and abroad; for peace and jobs; against wars and terrorism; and to bring our troops home.
>
> We support the rights of unions to bargain and the rights of undocumented workers to due process of law. We demand reform of our justice system to eliminate secret evidence and the consistent criminalization of inner-city communities.
>
> We support the rights of all people to practice their beliefs in peace at home and abroad, as well as equal opportunity for all. We ask Congress to conduct hearings against the rise of hate and hate groups in the United States.
>
> Together we urge that the untold billions of dollars now spent for wars instead be used for Americans' needs at home.

The 100 Imams emerged from the Muslim Peace Coalition, which was born in 2010 with a ferocious agenda. It is not one more platform for interfaith dialogue or to prove that Muslims are, after all, patriotic Americans. That kind of dross from the immediate aftermath of 9/11 held no water with the imams and their congregations who saw that such liberal feints were not sufficient protection from the onslaught of Islamophobia. A stronger brew was needed, and it came from the ferment of the anti-imperialist tradition. "The Muslim Peace Coalition believes that war, terrorism, and Islamophobia form a dangerous nexus that is dragging our nation backward," rings its founding statement. "It is not only our economy and constitution that are under attack because of this set, but our very spirit and morale, thus diminishing our standing as the world's leading nation." The last phrase ("world's leading nation") is a nod toward the discourse of patriotism, but it is not central to the practice of the Coalition, to its 100 Imams declaration, or to the antiwar platform that it has adopted: what is central is the nexus that it has identified between war, terrorism, and Islamophobia, or, in other words, between racism and imperialism.

By late October 2001, the American flags that were so ubiquitous across New York City left their half-mast positions and went back to the tops of the poles. The air in New York still smelled a little, and those of us who look like terrorists felt that we would perhaps never be able to shake the occasional suspicious glances and hostile remarks. In the world of South Asian America, organizing against this form of everyday terror began in earnest, with almost daily vigils, teach-ins, and other such activities set in motion. Meanwhile, those who organize the working-class immigrants (such as DRUM [Desis Rising

Up and Moving] and the New York Taxi Workers Alliance [NYTWA]) had a good sense of the backlash, and as it unfolded they understood precisely why it was happening and who was most vulnerable. DRUM and NYTWA were secular precursors of the 100 Imams, and they continue to operate alongside the recent public confidence of organized Islam. Taxi drivers, food vendors, convenience store owners, magazine kiosk workers—those who work in the public, and those who live in class/race-segregated neighborhoods (where the places of worship have become targets of violence)—were the people that bore the brunt of the assaults. Eighty-three thousand men complied with the government's Special Registration Program. Fourteen thousand went into deportation proceedings. Many thousands were deported for minor infractions. Their stories are generously collected in Irum Sheikh's *Detained Without Cause*.

Every bad side of history comes with its contradictions, and the South Asian American currents in organizations such as DRUM and NYTWA were alert to them. In the streets of New York, beside the flags and slogans of war, came posters that said "Food Not Bombs" and "More Violence Is Not Justice." Outside the Special Registration prisons and the deportation centers, the brave held vigils, and organizations like DRUM began to build a database of those who had disappeared into these prisons. Organizers such as Subhash Kateel, Aarti Shahani, and Shubh Mathur built DRUM's Detention Project, which was an essential part of the Coalition on Detention Incarceration, and then, after November 2002, Families for Freedom. "Grown uncles were crying on our voicemail," remembered Kateel.

BEFORE 9/11

Before 9/11 was 1993. When Ramzi Yousef and his confeder-
ates bombed the World Trade Center that year, a very gentle
tremor of fear spread through the communities of those who
might resemble terrorists. When I was in college in the 1980s,
a few unimaginative acquaintances would occasionally call me
"Qaddafi" (he was in the news a lot in that decade, having
been a burr under Ronald Reagan's saddle). People like me
had the misfortune of looking like your average terrorist: I had
a long pseudo-Afro in the 1980s, which provided the Qaddafi
look, and by the 1990s, I had the shorter-hair look that was au
courant among the terrorists who came from the Gulf. I've had
two bad-hair decades.

The general sentiment among Indian Americans was dis-
may. Racism against the olive skinned had begun to rise. (This
is reflected in the annual audits of the National Asian Pacific
American Legal Consortium; by 1998, 32 percent of all assaults on Asian Americans took place against South Asians,
compared to about 4.5 percent in 1995.) Inside the Indian
American community, which I knew best of all, the reactions
were diverse. Some had taken refuge in an idea that traveled
to them from India—that the hardened *Hindutva* Right was at
the high point of its campaign to transform Indian society from
secularism to sectarianism, with the "Muslim" as the target.
Drawing from this trend, some among the Indian Americans
tried to make the case that they were Hindus and not Muslims;
they wanted a "Get Out of Jail Free" card. Others dug deep
into their own careers and lives, hoping against hope that this
tide too would settle. And a few others began conversations

about profiling, linking the acute problem of racial profiling against blacks and Latinos by the police departments (as agents of the state) to the racial profiling against those who look like terrorists (not by the state but by society). These strategies provided respite, even if they ended up creating fissures between Hindus and Muslims. But they were not a sufficient respite.

The bombing of the Oklahoma federal building in 1995 by white supremacists was no comfort to Indian Americans, as it was no comfort to Arab Americans and Muslim Americans; the first reaction by the establishment press was that this was an act of violence by those who must be terrorists (Jim Stewart at CBS heard the news and went on the air to proclaim, "The betting here is on Middle East terrorists"). It turned out that this was more Midwest than Mideast, but that didn't stop the pundits (A.M. Rosenthal at the *New York Times* insisted, "Whatever we are doing to destroy Mideast terrorism, the chief terrorist threat against Americans, has not been working"). I remember a second sense of panic; the backlash was on the horizon. It would come six years later.

The sharp edge of 9/11 racism brought many among the migrants toward the politics of the South Asian Americans. They took refuge in the organizations created by South Asian Americans to counteract racism and xenophobia. "No one in my family talked much about racism when I was growing up," wrote Sonny Singh, reflecting on 9/11, "but suddenly it was clear that while many in my Sikh family might not share my anti-oppression leftist politics on paper, they sure as hell knew what it meant to be a target." SAALT and other organizations had previously created strong connections with the civil liberties and civil rights communities. SAALT was formed in 2000 to develop leadership among the community, with the intention of moving young people into mainstream American politics. The events of 9/11 changed SAALT, which began to do documentary work on anti–South Asian violence in the United States, making connections with Muslim and Arab organizations as well as East Asian organizations (whose own history regarding internment had brought them into the picture). SAALT produced two important documents to catalogue the violence and the sense of despondency and fear: a report on the violence (*American Backlash: Terrorists Bring War Home in More Ways Than One*, 2001) and a video of the community talking back (*Raising Our Voices: South Asian Americans Address Hate*, 2002). This was a genuine shift, bringing older and younger people into a political project to address overt and covert violence.

A few months before 9/11, SAALT's Deepa Iyer came to New York City to be part of a unique conference, Desis Organizing, put together by the city's progressive South Asian American organizations. Held in May, the conference intended, as lawyer activists Tito Sinha and Chaumtoli Huq reflected, "to build alliances and develop collaborative projects among the individuals and groups serving and organizing South Asian communities in the New York City metro area." A list of the organizations at Desis Organizing tells us a lot about the breadth of the interests and work being done: Agenda 21, Asian & Pacific Islander Coalition on HIV-AIDS, Asian/American Center at Queens College, Breakthrough, Chhaya CDC, Coalition of American Islamic Relations (CAIR), Desis Rising Up and Moving, New York Taxi Workers Alliance, NYU South Asian Law Students Association, Sakhi for South Asian

Women, Shakti Project, Sikh Mediawatch and Resource Task Force (SMART), SAALT, South Asian Journalists Association (SAJA), South Asian Lesbian and Gay Association (SALGA), South Asians Against Police Brutality and Racism, South Asian Action and Advocacy Collective (SAAAC), South Asian Women's Creative Collective (SAWCC), South Asian Youth Action (SAYA!), Telugu Association, Workers' Awaaz, and Youth Solidarity Summer (YSS). Reflecting on this conference ten years later, Dr. Nasir Gondal of CAIR noted, "This platform proved priceless a few months down the road when 9/11 happened. The immediate aftermath was most palpable in the South Asian community. It included the dragnet of detention, racial profiling, and a sense of overall helplessness and despair." The community organizers who were at Desis Organizing played an essential role in transforming the anxiety into action.

Over the course of the decade, SAALT changed its name to better reflect its new agenda (now South Asian Americans Leading Together) and formed the National Coalition of South Asian Organizations. Its members include the older South Asian women's organizations (Narika, Manavi, Sakhi) and the organizations formed in the aftermath of 9/11 (such as The Sikh Coalition), as well as more youth and community organizations with an eye to much more radical action (Desis Rising Up and Moving and South Asia Network). The political landscape changed dramatically from that of the 1990s. Attacks on Muslims and those who are mistaken for Muslim galvanized SAALT toward recognition of the domestic costs of imperial adventures. In the summer before the tenth anniversary of 9/11, SAALT conducted an "America for All of Us" campaign that resulted in the passage in Teaneck, New Jersey, of a farsighted antibias resolution by the city council, under the leadership of its mayor, Mohammed Hameeduddin. One becomes a part of the fabric of a country by being a part of its struggles, to make sure that its putative values do not ossify. Belonging does not come without a fight.

LONG-DISTANCE SOLIDARITY

The world derisively accosts us: O Coolie, O Coolie.
We have no fluttering flag of our own.
Our home is on fire.
Why don't we rise up and extinguish it?

—*Ghadar-di Gunj*, 1914

Fifteen years ago, I sat with Kartar Dhillon in her modest home in Berkeley, California. Kartar, who had lived a very full political life, told me about her brother, Budh. In 1924, twelve-year-old Budh marched down to 5 Wood Street in San Francisco, a building known as the Ghadar Ashram. There he volunteered to join a *jatha* to go and liberate India, a country that he had not yet visited. It was the homeland of his parents, and he told his sister that unless India was free, their lives in the United States would not be pleasant. People would treat them as coolies as long as India remained in British hands. Along with another teenager, Daswanda Singh Mann, Budh joined the Freedom for India Mission and set off across the Pacific Ocean. He did not get to India. En route through the young Soviet Union, Budh got distracted. The route into India was closed, so he enrolled in the University of Toilers of the East and learned a little bit about Marxism. Budh Dhillon returned to California and spent the rest of his life as an active militant for freedom and justice for all people.

Of such souls was the Ghadar Party made.

In 1913, veteran Indian nationalist Har Dayal used the $2,000 he had raised from Indian workers in California to buy a house in San Francisco. This house, the Yugantar Ashram initially, became the Ghadar Ashram, and it was from this base that Har Dayal began to publish a paper (initially 25,000 copies in Urdu). He named the newspaper *Ghadar* (Revolt), and its first issue (November 1, 1913) signaled its political views:

Wanted: Brave soldiers to stir up Ghadar in India.
Pay: Death.
Prize: Martyrdom.
Pension: Liberty.
Field of Battle: India.

A British intelligence agent who had his eyes on Har Dayal reported that by early January 1914, Indian students at Berkeley had hoarded arms (twenty revolvers and sixteen Winchester rifles). In 1922, the British Consulate in San Francisco reported, "California is gaining the reputation of a nursery for Revolution and Revolutionary agitators." When World War I broke out, Indians from along the western coast of North America went as if in an exodus toward India to fight British rule. Three Ghadar leaders—Ram Chandra, Bhagwan Singh, and Maulvi Mohammed Barkatullah—toured the West Coast to urge men to join the jathas and cultivate a revolution. A Ghadar song testified to the courage and the idealism of the returnees:

The time for prayer is gone.
It is time to take up the sword.
Empty talk does not serve any purpose.
It is time to engage in a fierce battle.
Only the names of those who long for martyrdom will shine.

The bulk of the Indian farmers and students who lived along the West Coast had deep-seated grievances against the British. Their families in India still suffered the indignities and extravagances of British rule, and these exiles continued to feel the stigma of exclusion and racism. The British Isles ruled the bulk of the colonized world, and in particular, a large share of the Indian subcontinent. Alert to the reach of British imperialism, Indian nationalists in the United States made common cause with the Irish republicans. Agnes Smedley, who worked for the Friends for the Freedom of India, wrote of her participation in New York's main Irish nationalist celebration in 1920, "We are in the St. Patrick's Day parade. All the Hindus in the city, practically, will wear native costume and turbans and march. We had the Indian republic flag and banners demanding independence." Both Ireland and India were held in thrall. The longest finger was pointed toward Britain.

Of the eight thousand emigrants who returned to India, four hundred were arrested by the British immediately, while twenty-five hundred more were interned in their villages. Their uprising did not come. Some of their best comrades (291 of them) stood in the dock in the Lahore Conspiracy Case; the bulk of them went to the gallows, or were sent to the Andaman Islands or to the Lahore jail. Idealistic, they came to inspire the

Indian army against their British masters. One among their lot, Prithvi Singh Azad, recalled their ethos: "The leaders of the Party in the U.S.A. were badly lacking in political awareness. We, a handful of people, plunged headlong in the field of action and had no mass support. We knew not how to gain mass support and never worked for that. We had been impelled by the impulse to free the nation from foreign yoke. I had been under the sway of a powerful passion to liberate my enslaved nation." Marxism was not available to them in a serious way (neither in India nor in the United States). As Maia Ramnath shows us in *Haj to Utopia*, the anarchists and syndicalists inspired many of these emigrants (Har Dayal's close confidant was the anarchist leader Emma Goldman, and many of the radicals worked alongside the International Workers of the World). They wanted to conduct spectacular acts, not organize the bulk of the population for a better world.

This was the milieu of Bhagat Singh, one of the most extraordinary freedom fighters of his generation. Alongside Bhagat Singh stood people like Prithvi Singh Azad and Sohan Singh Josh. Josh came from Chetanpura, Punjab, the same town as Surat Singh Gill. Both Gill and Josh had tried to go to the United States, but whereas Gill got a visa (and became Kartar Dhillon's husband), the U.S. embassy denied Josh. Josh grew up around Ghadarite radicals (and as a communist leader he would write an early history of the movement). It was through Josh that a young Bhagat Singh learned the history and theory of communism and Marxism. Ghadar, via the Soviet Revolution, played a central role in the dissemination of socialist and anti-imperialist ideas among the Punjabi youth.

Only marginally did the Ghadar workers turn their attention

to the role of U.S. imperialism and of Canadian complicity with British imperialism. The United States and Canada allowed the Indian radicals some space to work, although the governments also allowed British intelligence to follow their activities (our reconstruction of their work is made possible by these intelligence reports). When World War I broke out and many Indian radicals decided to make common cause with Germany, the United States and Canadian states went after them (M.N. Roy, for instance, fled to Mexico as a result of this pressure, where he helped found its Communist Party; he was the Mexican delegate to the Comintern meetings where he debated Lenin on the strategy for revolt in the colonial world). The repression provided the opportunity for some among the radicals to write in praise of the United States—that at the very least it had an ethos of republicanism and anticolonialism that Britain lacked. For example, Taraknath Das, Har Dayal's associate, wrote an essay for the Calcutta-based *Modern Review* entitled "American Diplomacy at Its Best," which extolled U.S. foreign policy. In 1950, Das wrote a note to the Indian government offering his analysis for how to operate in the United Nations. Here he wrote, "The United States has done more for Indian freedom than Britain and the Commonwealth could or can ever do. For India, cooperation with America remains of vital importance." It was the fear of communism and of Islam that distorted Das's otherwise commendable record in anticolonial work.

Most members of the Ghadar and other like organizations were well aware of U.S. imperialism. One of Har Dayal's close comrades was John Barry, a leader of the American Anti-Imperialist League (San Francisco branch) and of the Socialist

Radical Club. The League was formed in 1898 to oppose the United States annexation of Puerto Rico, Cuba, and the Philippines. "We hold that the policy known as imperialism is hostile to liberty and tends toward militarism, an evil which it has been our glory to be free," the League declared in its 1899 platform. "We regret that it has become necessary in the land of Washington and Lincoln to reaffirm that all men, of whatever race or color, are entitled to life, liberty, and the pursuit of happiness." Whereas the League took a strong position against imperialism, it promoted a grave illusion about the American Republic: that it had no prior history of expansionist activity. Forgotten in this was one of the causes of the 1776 War of Independence: for the settlers in the original thirteen colonies to expand westward. When they did, these settlers and their new state annihilated or pacified the Amerindian residents and annexed large parts of Mexico. Only when this proximate colonization was over did the United States exercise its right to the Western Hemisphere (through the 1823 Monroe Doctrine) and outward into the Pacific (the Hawaiian Islands and the Philippines).

If Har Dayal and others observed what was ongoing in Central America, they would have seen the future tendency of planetary imperialism. The U.S. government from 1915 onward began to absorb Caribbean islands (the Dominican Republic, Haiti, and Cuba) and parts of Central America (Nicaragua, Guatemala, and Panama) into its economic orbit by frequent military intervention and by the seizure of the economic sovereignty of these small countries. They were not ruled directly by the U.S. government, but their local satraps paid tribute to U.S. power (including U.S. corporations, such as the United Fruit

Company). No longer was imperialism identical with colonialism (for the extraction of resources and the creation of dependent markets); it had now threaded its tentacles into all areas of social life and economic accumulation. Foreign direct investment in Central and South America created a cumulative stock of investment, which in turn generated a return flow of earnings (as the U.S. Marxist Harry Magdoff argued in 1969). Nothing short of a broad united front against the structures of this form of imperialism would be adequate.

In 1915, the African American radical W.E.B. Du Bois (a close friend of many Indian nationalists) wrote an insightful essay, "The African Roots of the War." In this essay, Du Bois pointed out that the growth of monopoly capitalism alongside liberal democracy in Europe and North America led to the creation of a large quantum of surplus capital, some of which was turned over to the white working class (which became an aristocracy among labor). The uneven union of the white working class with their capitalist masters led, Du Bois argued, to an intranational fight over the world's spoils, mainly with the "darker nations of the world—Asia and Africa, South and Central America, the West Indies, and the Islands of the South Seas. The present world war," Du Bois continued, "is, then, the result of jealousies engendered by the recent rise of armed national associations of labor and capital whose aim is the exploitation of the wealth of the world mainly outside the European circle of nations. These associations, grown jealous and suspicious at the division of spoils of trade-empire, are fighting to enlarge their respective shares; they look for expansion, not in Europe but in Asia, and particularly in Africa." This argument would appear two years later, with slightly different emphases, in Lenin's *Imperialism*. Du Bois was greatly interested in developments in India, but his own writings were not to be regularly read by either the Indian political thinkers or the Indian radicals in the United States.

Only later, in the 1940s, would an Indian radical in the United States develop an understanding of the growth of U.S. imperialism. Kumar Goshal (born in 1899) had come to the United States in 1920 and, after a stint in Hollywood, became an ardent proponent of Indian independence (he was also close to the Communist Party in the United States). After 1947, Goshal became a main correspondent for the *Courier* (an African American paper in Pittsburgh), where he wrote an important three-part series in December 1953 called "People in Colonies Versus the American Colossus," where he lays out the contours of U.S. imperialism:

> To enlarge their empire during and since World War II, U.S. industrialists and financiers have knifed partners when partners were unable to retaliate; brought up or influenced governments through grants and loans; arranged 99-year leases for military bases on foreign soil; signed trade treaties giving U.S. capital "equal treatment" with weak domestic capital in economically backward countries; acquired air and naval bases in countries with weak or unpopular governments. No country is too small to escape the eye of U.S. corporations roaming the globe for more profits.

Not only did the United States put its considerable power and influence behind U.S.-based corporations, but it also found willing allies in the "darker nations" to do its bidding in the name of "modernization" and "democracy." U.S. imperialism was always smarter and more flexible than that of its European forebearers, who quickly became "American" in their own relationship to the rest of the world. Goshal was not known in India, but his line of analysis is not different from those communists who had few illusions about the Indian bourgeoisie and its tepid commitment to national sovereignty and to national development.

Goshal did not directly write about the links between domestic racism and imperialism. However, there is something poetic in his choice of subject and venue: he carved out a theory of U.S. imperialism in the African American press, largely the Pittsburgh *Courier*. It was to a readership aware of the full weight of Jim Crow that he elaborated his views on the emergence of a global Jim Crow under the tutelage of U.S. power. The U.S.-constructed and -run oil towns in Dhahran (Saudi Arabia) and Zulia (Venezuela) mimicked the racially segregated mining towns in Arizona and Colorado. The United States chose to praise pliant regimes, even when these were autocratic (Batista in Cuba), and it began a habit of overthrowing regimes that wanted to be independent (Árbenz in Guatemala). The uniforms of a new kind of empire (bases and docile governments) were being stitched and starched, but these uniforms borrowed heavily from customs of domestic hierarchy. These elements can be glimpsed in Goshal's writing, which laid out the similarities and differences between British imperialism, which he knew well as a child and as a journalist, and U.S. imperialism, which he knew as an adult and saw emerge before his own eyes.

Bhagat Singh's organization Naujawan Bharat Sabha wrote a farsighted manifesto in 1928 that exceeded the tactical, Ghadar-inspired struggle among these young people in India. "Without going into details," they wrote, "we can safely assert that to achieve our object, thousands of our most brilliant young men, like the Russian youth, will have to pass their precious lives in villages and make the people understand what the Indian revolution would really mean. They must be made to realize that the revolution that is to come will mean more than a change of masters. It will, above all, mean the birth of a new order of things, a new state." Political independence for India or social equality for Indian Americans was not sufficient. Imperial structures and imperial attitudes needed to be vanquished. It was a very tall but necessary order. Spectacular events were also not sufficient. What was needed was sacrifice, hard work, and patience.

Three years later, from Central Jail Lahore, Bhagat Singh wrote his letter to political workers. He asked them to form a Communist Party and to begin their ceaseless work among the masses to create a popular will for socialism. In this brief essay, Bhagat Singh returned to the origins of Punjabi radicalism, the Ghadar. "One of the fundamental causes of the failure of the efforts of the Ghadar Party (1914–15)," he wrote, "was the ignorance, apathy, and sometimes active opposition of the masses. And apart from that, [an organized party] is essential for gaining the active sympathy of and organizing the peasants and workers." By "ignorance" Bhagat Singh did not mean stupidity as much as lack of access to a broader analysis of oppression and exploitation. This is what an organized movement in constant struggle against power can produce; struggle is, in his own words, a school for the masses.

As Bhagat Singh waited in jail, a second group of Ghadar Party radicals entered India. They came with a different purpose. Harbans Singh Basi, Bhagat Singh Bilga, Iqbal Singh Hundal, Chanan Singh, Gurmukh Singh, Prithvi Singh, Teja Singh Swatantar, and others came from Moscow not to conduct individual acts of violence or to hope for an uprising in the army. They returned to build the Indian Communist Party.

Abject subjects of the British Empire, the overseas Indians in the 1910s and the 1920s at least recognized that they would not be treated as human beings as long as their homelands remained in bondage. That was established by the emergence of the Ghadar Party in Stockton, California, in 1913. They knew that there was a link between their own social standing and social identity and that of the foreign policy of the nation-state in which they lived. The U.S. government and its people would regard Indians as coolies as long as the British had dominion over South Asia. It is this link between foreign policy and social life that has not held fast over the century. Today many migrants believe that they can simply walk away from their homelands and rebuild their lives and identities in their new lands. This is simply not possible. The miasma of international relations interrupts our lives constantly.

Since 9/11, the concord between the generations has emerged slowly, but surely, in the world of U.S. domestic politics. Technical and professional migrants join with their well-educated children to bemoan the racism they too recognize. Often they join with working-class and lower-middle-class migrants if the platform that they share simply puts forward the liberal plea to be treated as humans and not as terrorists.

This is a vision that does not extend to a condemnation of an Islamophobia that increasingly seems to have taken the place of communism as the bogey of bourgeois liberalism.

Absent links to working-class and lower-middle-class migrants and to all those who recognize that there is little that divides the disgust at the olive-skinned from Islamophobia, a mass platform is unavailable to Indian Americans and South Asian Americans. But even in each of these spaces, there is barely any place to develop an argument on the dilemmas of international relations in the subcontinent and in the Arab world. Some of this has to do with varying state interests in South Asia, with those from India perhaps unwilling to take the view of those from Pakistan, and vice versa. Such distinctions make it hard to hold even a bare minimum of common understanding of the problems in South Asia and in the region around it. Nor is there much agreement on the causes of terrorism, as Dick Cheney's maxim ("one person's terrorist is another person's freedom fighter") remains alive and well. Imputed disagreements such as these make most organizations afraid to even try to forge a common understanding; why start something that you think is fated to fail?

If the Ghadar militants wanted India to be free for their dignity, the Indian Americans of the 1990s and early 2000s wanted the Indian economy to "shine" as a way to be proud Indian Americans. Any talk of poverty or agrarian collapse chafed against this tendency. It meant, of course, that one could have no serious discussion about the rise of the political Right, which has rested its claims on the dissatisfaction of the bulk of the population and which now twists its exploitative message to promote the belief that the path to a full belly is through the mosque or the temple. No real consideration of terrorist violence is possible without a serious conversation about the kind of economic policy pushed by the many Indians and Indian Americans who work at places like the World Bank, the International Monetary Fund, Goldman Sachs, Pfizer, Pepsi, and so on. Eagerness to cement close ties between India and the United States has meant, in the context of the increasing corporate power in the United States and India, disavowing any criticism of the perilous corporate and military ties between the two countries. Much the same has occurred between Pakistan and the United States, with the obsession with a military solution to al-Qaeda and Afghanistan-Pakistan (Af-Pak) driving the United States into a lethal dependence on the Pakistani military.

In truth, 9/11 is all about foreign policy. Its aftermath inside the United States affected desis, who then forged responses of various kinds to racism and profiling. Little was done for the root problem: the exertion of U.S. power into the lands that stretch from the western Sahara to the Philippines. The 9/11 racism is a symptom of a much deeper problem. Neither the Indian Americans nor the South Asian Americans seem prepared to deal with that much-graver issue, the overreach of American power into the Asiatic heartlands. We've been able to acknowledge the hurdle of race; the next hurdle is imperialism. If we don't see it, and work on it, racism—a consequence of imperialism—will persist. That's the message of Ghadar, and it resonates.

3

The India Lobby

Zara mulk ke rahbaron ko bulaao
Ye kooche, ye galiyaan, ye manzar dikhaao
Jinhen naaz hai Hind par unko laao
Jinhen naaz hai Hind par voh kahaan hai?

Go, fetch the leaders of the nation
Show them these streets, these lanes, these sights
Summon them, those who are proud of India
Those who are proud of India, where are they?

— Sahir Ludhianvi, *Pyaasa*, 1957

Gopal Raju, who died in 2008 at the age of eighty, was impatient to put Indian Americans on the map. The founder of the community's most popular newspaper, *India Abroad*, Raju wanted to provide a platform for Indian Americans to exercise power in Washington, D.C. I met him in the early 1990s, right around the time he founded the Indian American Center for Political Action (IACPA). The center drew in young Indian Americans born to parents who came to the country after the 1965 revision of the immigration laws. In college, many of them rediscovered their ethnic history, not so much as the cultural quotient of their suburban youth, but now as a political identity produced by college multiculturalism. Their various dilemmas of place and identity had to be suborned to the compulsions of the first generation—namely, boosting India and the agenda of its government in the hallways of D.C.

Raju recruited these young people as interns and sent them off to work for members of Congress, most of whom had until now little concern for India, let alone Indian America. Raju's dream was elegant: American Jews (7 million) make up only about 2.5 percent of the U.S. population, and yet they are able to influence U.S. policy toward Israel; if only Indian Americans (whose demography resembles that of American Jews) could also have such an impact. Raju could have been inspired by the Cuban example, with only 1.6 million in the United States (0.5 percent of the population), but after the Bay of Pigs and a few isolated terrorist acts, Cuban Americans have been rather unimpressive, the embargo notwithstanding. The Israel Lobby, on the other hand, has made the United States into "Israel's attorney" (according to former U.S. State Department official Aaron David Miller). This is what impressed Raju and those who followed him.

For his expertise along these lines, Raju hired Ralph Nurnberger, who had played a very significant role in the American Israel Public Affairs Committee (AIPAC). But Raju's dream was simply pragmatic: he had no special fealty to Israel nor did he labor under the illusion of a special relationship between Hindus and Jews. "If they can do it," he told me, "we can too."

Scores of young Indian Americans flooded the antechambers of congressional leaders, just as the Indian government decided it too needed to have a closer, even special, relationship with Washington, D.C. From the early 1990s, the Indian government decided to abandon any pretense of nonalignment and to seek Washington's favor. It gradually dismantled its protection of the Indian economy, leaned toward Tel Aviv for the first time, and backed away from too close an association with the nonaligned movement. All this sent a signal to Washington that Delhi wanted its intimacy. The Indian Embassy welcomed the IACPA initiative, but it had its own irons in the fire. Until 1992, India's government had made it a point to send retired Foreign Service members (M.C. Chagla) or prominent people in need of a sinecure (Karan Singh) to be ambassadors to the United States. Those with eminence, such as Vijaya Lakshmi Pandit and T.N. Kaul, looked more favorably to Moscow or to the capitals of Africa and Asia than to the White House. In 1992, the Indian government sent an energetic anticommunist and pro-Washington politician, Siddhartha Shankar Ray, to move an agenda. Ray went all out, making controversial public comments against members of the U.S. Congress who had taken an adverse position on human rights violations in India, and publicly asking for the reelection of a senator favorable to India, Larry Pressler of South Dakota. At a news conference, the Indian minister of state for foreign affairs, R.L. Bhatia, said, "There is a strong anti-India lobby in the United States. We are spending large sums of money through Ambassador Ray to neutralize it." Ray also recognized the importance of the Indian American community, which by the early 1990s had established itself in the worlds of technology and finance. Ray took his orders from the Parliamentary Standing Committee on External Affairs, which asked the Indian diaspora to "help in projecting India in proper perspective" and to "neutralize the hostile propaganda abroad." It was in this light that Ray urged Indian Americans to "get more involved in advancing not only their own interests but also that of the Motherland." Gopal Raju heard that message loud and clear. His young troops were already in the field.

Nudged by the emergent Indian American community and by the newfound business opportunities in India, members of the U.S. Congress hastily created an India Caucus in December 1992. Democratic congressmen Stephen Solarz and Frank Pallone led the way, but the initial enthusiasm was limited (only eight joined up, one of them a Republican). Solarz, from Staten Island, New York, and Pallone, from New Jersey's Sixth District, both had substantial Indian American constituents (Pallone's district included Edison, 20 percent of whose population was Indian American and therefore, rightly, the capital of Indian America). Pallone recognized that this ethnic bloc needed to be cultivated, and he proceeded with finesse. The Indian government had recently begun to "liberalize" its economy; it had opened its arms toward Israel, and, with Ray's appointment as ambassador, it had signaled that it wanted a new relationship with the United States. Pallone became the go-to guy, and in under a decade he brought more than a quarter of the House to the India Caucus. It helped, of course, that the Indian American community had money in its pocket and its "leaders" (those with the money) wanted to be players in D.C. The India Lobby tested its mettle by destroying the annual move by Indiana's Dan Burton to end U.S. assistance to India. Burton eventually said that the India Lobby "beat me into the ground." No loss there, really. In 2002, Pallone won one of India's highest civilian awards, the Padma Bhushan. Winning the award with Pallone was Gary Ackerman of New York, who took over chairmanship of the Caucus from Pallone. Two decades later, the India Caucus in the 110th House of Representatives includes 180 members, and the Senate's Caucus (formed in 2004) has about thirty-seven senators. The India Caucus is the largest country-group in the House.

To stiffen the spine of the caucuses and give them their talking points, the Indian government has, over the past decade, hired a number of lobbying organizations—the Berman Group, the Washington Group, and American Continental. None of this was serious until 1998, when the government finally grasped the nettle and hired its old friend Stephen Solarz and his APCO firm (to hedge its bets, the government also hired the more Republican-oriented Verner, Lipfert, Bernhard, McPherson and Hand). Since 2008, the Indian government has been represented by K Street's finest: Barbour, Griffith & Rogers as well as Patton, Boggs. In March 2009, Patton, Boggs hired former U.S. ambassador to India Frank Wisner Jr. to lay claim to the India desk after his controversial service in India. During his tenure in New Delhi, Wisner put all his resources toward helping Enron win the right to build the elephantine Dabhol power plant. One of his staffers said of these resources, "If anybody asked the CIA to help promote U.S. business in India, it was probably Frank."

When Wisner left India, he joined the board of Enron. He illustrates well the close links between government and business. No wonder, then, that it would be Wisner who joined the firm to work "discreetly" to further the interests of the Indian government and the U.S.-India business networks, including the two major Indian commercial organizations (the

Federation of Indian Chambers of Commerce and the Con-
federation of Indian Industry), the U.S.-India Institute, and the
newly revived U.S.-India Business Council.

U.S.-based corporations saw an immediate asset in closer
ties between the United States and India. In the early 1990s,
the U.S. administration read the shift in India quite correctly.
Treasury Secretary Lloyd Bentsen observed the middle class of
60 million—the size of France—and salivated. For Bentsen,
and for the Clinton administration, the existence of this class
and its hitherto suffocated desires meant that there existed a
market to help contain the crisis of overaccumulation to which
"globalization" was to be the answer. A decline in the annual
rate of growth of the global Gross Domestic Product from the
1960s (5.4 percent) to the 1980s (3 percent) offered evidence
of the crisis, but nothing was as stark as the falling profit rate of
the top 500 U.S. transnational corporations (4.7 percent in the
late 1950s to -5.3 percent in the 1980s). Walden Bello recites
these figures and concludes, "Oversupply of commodities and
inadequate demand are the principal corporate anomalies in-
hibiting performance in the global economy." Bentsen's comments had a concrete purpose: the U.S. administration hoped,
in essence, that India's middle class might absorb this oversupply. The Indian government began a long process to dismantle
various kinds of social protections for both the national economy and for the dispossessed and exploited classes. This process did not come easily, since the newly confident dominant
classes in India had yet to settle accounts with the powerful
institutions of the working class and peasantry (trade unions,
political parties, sociopolitical organizations, peasant groups,
and so on). Nevertheless, by 1994, large sections of industrial

production, the extraction sector, utilities, transportation, tele-communications, and finance found themselves prey to private investors.

In the 1990s in Washington, D.C., the U.S.-India Business Council (USIBC) emerged out of hibernation (it was founded in 1975) to lobby for business interests in India and for the reconfiguration of the Indian economy to favor business over social needs. Under Karen Swaner, Michael Clark, and then Ron Somers (from 2004), the USIBC galvanized the corporate sector to take an interest in developments within India. Secretary of Commerce Ron Brown took twenty-five private-sector CEOs to India in 1995, a visit that launched the U.S.-India Commerce Alliance to promote trade and investment between corporate entities on both shores. Somers came to USIBC from the energy industry, one of the main arenas of interest for U.S. firms as India's inexhaustible energy needs would be unfurled by the new growth-oriented economy. The USIBC is housed, conveniently, in the U.S. Chamber of Commerce building in Washington, from where it pushes against the walls erected in India to protect the national economy from those who want to make dollars out of rupees.

The springboard for the USIBC has been the U.S.-India nuclear deal. Eager to bring India on board against Iran, the Bush administration hastily offered to forgive India for the nuclear tests of 1998, provide it with diplomatic cover to gain favor in the Nuclear Suppliers Group, and open the doors to technology for the development of nuclear energy systems. In gratitude, India was to forgo the "peace pipeline" to run from Iran to India via Pakistan, and it was to offer its diplomatic weight against Iran in the International Atomic Energy Agency. As

U.S. ambassador to India David Mulford told India's foreign secretary Shyam Saran in 2005, members of the U.S. Congress "were watching India's treatment of Iran prior to congressional debate on the U.S.-India civilian nuclear initiative." For the nuclear deal, the USIBC and the U.S. Chamber of Commerce's Coalition for Partnership with India drew upon the lobbying expertise of Patton, Boggs and Stonebridge International. They had a vested interest in the deal, because it would have allowed U.S. firms to gain contracts in the Indian nuclear sector. In March 2007, the USIBC hosted a 230-member business delegation to India, the Commercial Nuclear Executive Mission. Tim Richards of General Electric (GE) gingerly said of the trip, "We know India's need for nuclear power." (There is, in fact, no such imperative; as energy analyst Prabir Purkayastha puts it, nuclear power would cover a maximum of only 7 percent of India's energy needs.) Ron Somers, president of USIBC, said of the purported $60 billion boondoggle that would have come as a result of the deal, "The bounty is enormous." Somers's comment did not please his friends in the nuclear commerce world. They wanted the deal to go through (as it did in 2008) quietly. As GE India's chief executive officer T.P. Chopra told a Wharton periodical, "The last thing we want is to give ammunition to the Left-wing parties. They would love to project the U.S. as greedy capitalists selling the country for a few dollars more. Business will keep silent until it's signed, sealed and delivered."

The India Lobby had a harder time with the problem of outsourcing. Princeton economist Alan Blinder's "Offshoring: the New Industrial Revolution?" (*Foreign Affairs*, March/April 2006) explores the extent of the problem. "We have so far barely seen the tip of the offshoring iceberg," he writes, "the eventual dimensions of which may be staggering." In our time, manufacturing jobs have been exported out of the United States at an alarming rate for workers, while service jobs have only begun to disappear. "The fraction of service jobs in the United States and other rich countries that can potentially be moved offshore is certain to rise as technology improves and as countries such as China and India continue to modernize, prosper, and educate their work forces," Blinder says. "Eventually, the number of service-sector jobs that will be vulnerable to competition from abroad will likely exceed the total number of manufacturing jobs. Thus, coping with foreign competition, currently a concern for only a minority of workers in rich countries, will become a major concern for many more." Blinder is right about what outsourcing is doing to the capacity of U.S. job creation, but he exaggerates its benefits to India. In India, the IT sector, for example, is an enclave that employs fewer than a million workers. It is not the center of things.

The word "India" now refers in many quarters to outsourcing. On his radio show, Ed Schulz joked that if you call customer service, you get a guy named Ralph on the phone. "What he means is Rajiv," Schulz laughed. NBC briefly ran a sitcom called *Outsourced*, which followed the travails of Todd Dempsey, who preferred to relocate to India than get fired. He trains his Indian call center colleagues in the ways of America. On NBC, the show followed *The Office*, which is an American adaptation of the successful British comedy. *The Office* is an anxiety-ridden show in which the pathetic characters glide between comedic shenanigans and the horror of being laid off.

Outsourced picked up the thread right after *The Office* ended, and it took us to the outer limits of disquiet for the white-collar American worker.

In 2005, while on a trip to India, then-senator Hillary Clinton told a meeting of industrialists, "There is no way to legislate against reality. Outsourcing will continue." By her estimates, the United States exported $5 billion in merchandise to India, and India exported $13.8 billion to the United States. (The World Trade Organization cites far lower figures for Indian exports, somewhere closer to half this number). This unevenness does not sit well in the United States. "I have to be frank," she told the business leaders. "People in my country are losing their jobs and the U.S. policy makers need to address this issue." Her suggestion was that "Indian companies should invest more in the U.S. to create a balance in trade relations." The showcase for this is a small office opened by Tata Consultancy Services in Buffalo, New York.

But Senator Clinton is not alone in her defense of outsourcing. The Democratic Party is broadly committed to outsourcing, although with a caveat: it does not "believe in tax giveaways that reward companies for moving American jobs overseas." But it will not do anything to halt the hemorrhaging of jobs. In June 2008, Barack Obama's campaign for president released a tasteless memo calling Clinton the senator from Punjab, quoting Rajwant Singh at a Maryland fund-raiser (Singh had said that she was popular enough to be senator in both New York and Punjab). But this was all political theater. Obama had no plan either. Nor did the Republicans. The logic of cost and the advantages of technology continue to export jobs overseas (not necessarily to India, as they did not necessarily go to Ireland before that). Capital is not patriotic. It seeks out the maximum return. India just happens to fit the bill at present.

The issue of outsourcing is at a resentful simmer, and it returned once more after the credit crunch of 2007. The new unemployed, who have joined the disposable working class in a structural sense but not at all in a subjective sense, are white-collar managerial workers who inhabit the office parks answering phones, managing inventory, and straightening up databases. With the new information technology, secure communication lines, and the lower wages of India and China, these white-collar jobs have begun to disappear from the suburban enclaves where they had grown. The foreclosure epidemic hit their neighborhoods, where edifice envy now crumbles into cashless anxiety. These new jobless did not expect to lose their jobs; their sense of entitlement is fierce, grounded in imperial and racial advantages. Unlike the industrial working class, they know how to use the system and are kindling for the kind of rhetoric of Sarah Palin and Glenn Beck, Michelle Bachmann and Bill O'Reilly. One Tea Party member wrote, "Outsourcing is a pit that America needs to climb out of." At the bottom of the pit is India. Large sections of the Lobby favor outsourcing because it is what corporations want, and because they believe it benefits India. Neither the Lobby nor the Outsourcer has any interest in the *people* and their needs. Profit governs their worldview.

Guns didn't stand too far away from butter. In September 1994, India's army chief, General B.C. Joshi, visited the top U.S. army brass and Secretary of Defense William Perry.

Ententes signed, the two armed forces began to train together to secure what in military theory is known as "interoperability." The Indian and U.S. navies held several exercises whose natural outgrowth has been the joint patrols in the waters around India, from Singapore to Somalia. (It was an Indian warship, the *INS Tabar*, that sank a Somali pirate vessel in November 2008.) Arms shipments went to India, and Indian officers flew to the United States for training. The U.S. military was keen on having a contingent of Indian troops in Iraq, but the Communists and wizened nationalists in the Congress Party blocked the request in 2003. During Obama's 2010 visit to India, Thom Hartmann, the progressive radio show host, reported that Obama had cut billions of dollars in deals with India. He noted that Obama said that these deals would create jobs in the United States. This amused him. Hartmann pointed out that very little is produced in America. One premium product is weaponry, so no wonder that a large part of the trade deals that are cut are for India to buy U.S. weapons. This is not far from the truth. In 2010, the United States inked a $60.5 billion arms deal with Saudi Arabia. The deals with India will not amount to as much, though they will simply add to the mammoth total. The arms industry that is spread across the congressional districts of the United States will hum. The work will not be outsourced; it defines what remains of manufacturing in the United States.

This is the "official" India Lobby: its muscle came out in 2009 when it squelched any attempt to include India and Kashmir in special envoy Richard Holbrooke's brief. When the Obama team broached the subject of Bill Clinton as an India envoy, the Lobby went apoplectic: it neither wanted Kashmir to become an international issue (India sees it as a bilateral matter between it and Pakistan) nor did it want to be associated with other "problem areas," such as Israel-Palestine, Iran, and Afghanistan-Pakistan. The Lobby had its way.

4

How the Hindus Became Jews

On the Hindu side there is the appreciation that a Zionist Palestine may be an important link in the defense policy of India, that it may, with the support of European nations, be an
effective counter-weight to an alliance of Islamic countries in
the Middle East and in the third place that between Hinduism
and Judaism there is a great deal in common in the matter of
culture.

—K.M. Panikkar, diplomat, April 8, 1947,
Central Zionist Archives, S25/9092

Rumors flew that the Indian Embassy in Washington asked its
nationals to wear a *bindi* to help distinguish "Indians" from
Arabs and Afghans. *Outlook* magazine reported in October
2011, "In this atmosphere thick with fear, talk that the Indian
embassy had asked Indian women to use the bindi—to identify
themselves as not Arab or Afghan—got around fast. The embassy, of course, denies it ever issued any such directive." A gay
friend called to say that this was the first time that he knew of
the Indian government asking its male citizens to adopt drag.
Another friend bitterly mentioned that the bindi had once

stirred resentment against desis, at least in the 1980s, when
the Dotbusters of New Jersey began a hate campaign against
Indian immigrants. Now that Madonna had made the bindi
fashionable, the rumor mills had begun to offer it as protection
against the revanchism that followed 9/11. Talk of the bindi
went about as a way for some to suggest it as an adequate sign
of being a Hindu, or at least not a Muslim.

Some Indian Americans sought shelter from this storm not
so much in the category of "whiteness," but in an attempt to
manufacture an alliance with Jewish American organizations.
The game for this set of influential Indian Americans was to
see in Jewish Americans a model for their own attempt not simply to gain respectability in mainstream America, but to gain
power in Washington. These are the "Hindus" who want to re-
pudiate the hundreds of millions of Muslims in South Asia, to
create an image of the Indian as a victim of Muslim terrorism
in South Asia, and therefore the Indian American's dilemma as
akin to the Jewish American's distress over "Muslim" terrorism
in Israel. That those who operate with terrorist means are not
simply Muslims is the exact idea that had to be demolished,
because what allowed "Hindus" and "Jews" to become kin re-
lied principally on the reduction of Palestinians and Kashmiris
and Gujaratis to "Muslim."

"Hindu" is not a coherent entity, rent as it is not only by
theological disputes but also by many political disagreements
as well as the everyday divides of gender, class, and caste. But
there is a far more particular reason for the tentativeness of
these terms. If we run three of the terms in sequence (Jewish-
Hindu-Muslim), one point is revealed: they are no longer terms
that define only religions or religious experience. "Muslim"

has come to refer to a global community of Muslims who ad-
here to a singular theocratic ideology (Islam), reinforced by a
clergy that interprets a single book (the Koran). The varieties of
religious experience within the Islamic community are rarely
acknowledged, or else very rarely explored by the uninitiated.
The term "Jewish" has come to refer less to religion and more
to culture. We assume that regardless of their political or theological commitments, all those who are born in a Jewish family
are Jews because of the culture of Judaism. The association of
something called "Jewish culture" enables conservative activists of the Hindu Right to claim that regardless of one's religion
or politics, any Indian is culturally a Hindu. Hindu culture, in
this logic, is like Jewish culture, and the idea of a modular form
of a religious culture being the culture of a people circumvents
any suggestion of diversity within the category: all those who
are Indian are part of Hindu culture, even if they are not Hindus, and Jews are always Jews because, despite their religious
and political differences, they exist within Jewish culture. If
"Muslims" form part of the global community of Islam, then
Indian Muslims are more Muslim than Indian; if all those of
India are Hindus, then Indian Muslims are Hindus when they
deny their place in the global community of Islam.

Events and processes that appear to be fundamentally
outside the story of the United States, at least after 9/11, are
a fundamental component of domestic race and racism. It is
my contention that race in the United States after 9/11 has to
be seen on a global scale, because planetary events lean upon
the social construction and reconfiguration of identity within
the United States. Jewish American identity has, at least since
1967, been in direct contact with the place of Israel in world

affairs, and since 9/11, the importance of the links between India and Israel have fashioned one section of the desi community. Race in the United States is constructed with an eye to global events. In my own earlier work I argued that the fear factor of "blacks" created the conditions for the construction of the Indian American (and the Asian American in general) as the model minority, whereas now I will argue that this is insufficient. It is the terror factor of the "Muslim" alongside antiblack racism that provides the political space for Jewish Americans and Indian (or sometimes Hindu) Americans to mitigate their cultural difference from the mainstream, but crucially to put themselves forward as those who, because of their experience with terrorism, become the vanguard of the new, antiterrorist Battleship America.

THE LOTUS AND THE UZI

If you go in search of the headquarters of the Research and Analysis Wing (India's CIA), you will find it behind a small tea shop. If you can't find the tea shop as you wind your way around Lodhi Road, ask anyone. They'll tell you that the tea shop is right in front of the RAW headquarters.

In the mid-1990s, an old friend worked at RAW. I asked him about the new language of security that seemed to overshadow the older language of development and poverty alleviation, of socialism and nonalignment. "Look at Israel," he said. "They have the answers for us. Why should we tolerate what the Pakistanis dole out? We need to hit them hard. That's the Israel road." But what about the level of insecurity within Israel, I asked him; it seemed to me that the Israeli road had *failed* to provide security to its own people. Israel's most remarkable achievement has been to sell its failure to attain peace as a counterterrorist success story. What was there to emulate? But my friend had absorbed the grammar of hot pursuit, targeted assassination, and security border walls. In 1992, Likud's Binyamin Netanyahu bragged that Israel had "developed expertise in dealing with terrorism at the field level and also internationally at the political and legal level, and would be happy to share it with India." The context of political disagreements within Kashmir or along the India-Pakistan border faded from sight as the problem became framed around ideas of "terrorism" and "security." The logic of force overwhelmed the arguments for more discourse. It was claustrophobic.

The boss of the Indian Right, L.K. Advani (one of the main champions of Hindutva, or political Hinduism), had extended a hand to his doppelgänger, Netanyahu. In 2000, when Advani was the home minister, he traveled to Israel and told a gathering at the Indian Embassy, "In recent years we have been facing a growing internal security problem. We are concerned with cross-border terrorism launched by proxies of Pakistan. We share with Israel a common perception of terrorism as a menace, even more so when coupled with religious fundamentalism. Our mutual determination to combat terrorism is the basis for discussions with Israel, whose reputation in dealing with such problems is quite successful." Israeli counterterrorism teams came to India alongside Israeli arms merchants. India is now the largest single importer of Israeli weaponry.

On April 20, 2000, the Indian Space Research Organisation launched an Israeli spy satellite, RISAT-2, after the January launch of TECSAR, another such satellite. The technocrats of terrorism set aside all consideration of the local political dimensions of the conflicts and the considerable commonalities between India and Pakistan that could be the foundation for a durable peace. Instead, the conflict is seen as permanent, and the issue at hand is how to strengthen the technologies of power in India in order to contain Pakistan's hand as well as the many tentacles of the terror outfits. Imports of capital-intensive weaponry impressed the Indian middle class, which had itself only just come out from under the obligations of *dirigisme*, a middle class eager to model itself after the debt-laden middle classes of the advanced industrial states, whose own idea of security was a scaled-up version of the gated community.

The arms deals escalate. It is hard to keep up with them, not only because their various domains seem to multiply, from small arms to space weaponry, but also because the governments on both sides are loath to go public about them. In February 2008, Israel's ambassador to India, Mark Sofer, told *Outlook*, "We do have a defense relationship with India, which is no secret. On the other hand, what is a secret is what is the defense relationship. And with all due respect, the secret part of it will remain secret." Two years later, Mani Shankar Aiyer, a member of the Indian parliament, told the *Indian Express*, "We have become so dependent on defense supplies from Israel that when I put up a Rajya Sabha question seeking the government to reply on whether it equated the large numbers of civilians killed by Israeli forces in Gaza Strip—as found by the Goldstone fact-finding team—with the killings of Hamas, the External Affairs disallowed my question, calling it a state secret. Since when has the subject of India-Palestine relations

become a state secret given the fact that India was in the forefront of the Palestinian struggle?"

Before 9/11, *Jane's Terrorism and Security Monitor* noted,
"Israeli intelligence agencies have been intensifying their relations with the Indian security apparatus and are now understood to be heavily involved in helping New Delhi combat
Islamic militants in the disputed province of Kashmir." By February 2003, reports had come that the Indian government had
sent at least three battalions of its crack troops to be trained
in anti-insurgency operations in Israel. By 2010, a young Turk
in the Indian Congress Party Jyotiraditya Scindia, who comes
from a former royal family, greeted Israel's Shimon Peres with
what would become the usual pablum (India and Israel share
a "relationship between two souls"), but then got down to business. "Israel's homeland security systems are way ahead and
India can benefit from your own experience. We have to co-
operate to the fullest extent to combat the menace." He didn't
spell out fully what he considered the "menace," but the impli-
cation seemed clear enough.

On September 8, 2003, Israeli prime minister Ariel Sharon
arrived in New Delhi to spend the second anniversary of 9/11
with his Indian counterpart. This was the first visit by an Israeli
prime minister in India's five-decade history, and it came at
a propitious time. Right-wing governments ruled in Tel Aviv,
New Delhi, and Washington, and they wanted to form an alliance. No surprise that on 9/11 itself, Israel's national security
advisor and former head of the National Security Institute, Major General Uzi Dayan, was in New Delhi, meeting with the
RAW officials. Dayan praised the "special strategic relation"

between the two countries. This was a relation that exceeded
the massive arms deals; it was a relation that revolved around
a shared ideological and strategic vision: a fear and hatred of
what they understood as a common adversary, what they called
Islamic terrorism.

THE HINDU LOBBY

The telephone calls were sinister. Threats to body combined
with unkind things about my family. Reference was made to
my being a fraudulent Hindu, perhaps even a secret Muslim.
What guided these intrepid callers was a website with a "hit
list," run by Rohit Vyasmaan, a rather mysterious man who
lived in the greater New York area (it is at www.hinduunity
.com). The page had my phone number and my home address.
I called the local police; they pleaded helplessness. Telephone
calls to the Internet provider led to the site's dismissal. And
then something interesting happened. This website was run
by the overseas wing of the most virulent strand of political
Hinduism, the Bajrang Dal. Not long after its Internet exile, it
was welcomed back thanks to the good fortune of the network
established by the followers of the Rabbi Meir David Kahane.
Vyasmaan, who is often called the leader of Hindu unity, con-
sented to an interview with the New York Times in 2002, telling
the reporter, "We are fighting the same war. Whether you call
them Palestinians, Afghans, or Pakistanis, the root of the problem for Hindus and Jews is Islam."

Not far from these extreme forces, across the Hudson River
in New Jersey, other Jewish American and Indian American groups began to meet formally in the months after 9/11.

Shaken by 9/11, and drawing analogies between that attack and events as far removed as the Indian partition and the current imbroglio in Kashmir, well-connected Indian Americans reached out to their friends in the American Jewish Committee (AJC) and AIPAC. Most of the activists were in their midthirties; many of them had come to the United States for college or as very young children, and the bulk of them were given over to the Republican Party: Jesal Amin, Sue Ghosh Stricklett, and Sanjay Puri all fit this basic profile. They founded what would become USINPAC (the U.S. India Political Action Committee), a group that owed its legs to the Israel Lobby (Ann Schaffer of AJC said of this connection, "We shared with them the Jewish approach to political activism. We want to give them the tools to further their political agenda"). It turns out that "their political agenda" is not so different from that of the Israel Lobby. As Ghosh Stricklett, USINPAC's defense and strategic affairs point person, put it in 2004, "Our no. 1 legislative priority is terrorism: the terrorism directed against India is the same as that directed against the United States and Israel." That terrorism, Congressman Tom Lantos (now deceased) told an Indian American gathering, is "mindless, vicious, fanatic, Islamic terrorism." The only answer to this "mindless" terrorism is to fumigate it.

Lantos had an electoral prejudice toward Indian Americans. They comprised a significant section of the wealthy in his district (California's Twelfth), which included large parts of the Silicon Valley. As militant as Lantos was Gary Ackerman (of New York's Fifth, including Queens, home to a large number of Indian Americans). Ackerman helped coordinate the links between AIPAC, AJC, and USINPAC. Israel, he said, is "surrounded by 120 million Muslims," whereas "India has 120 million" Muslims within. These 120 million each posed a threat to the two countries he admired. They needed help maintaining U.S. assistance in the war against 240 million people. In 1999, Ackerman was in Atlanta at an Indian American event where he celebrated the "ancient civilizations" of Hindus and Jews, pointing out that "Strong India-Israel relations is very critical to ensuring peace and stability in a part of the world that is characterized by instability, fundamentalist religious bigotry, hatred toward the West and its values, and murder and mayhem spawned by acts of cross-border terrorism." Such a reductive vision of North Africa, the Middle East, and South Asia is remarkable for its surety: the richness of the entire belt collapses into the anomie that must lead to a foreign policy ruled by guns and garrisons. In 2001, Ackerman's legislative aide, Narayan Keshavan, said, "There are scores of congressmen and dozens of senators who clearly equate the growing Indian American political influence to the 'Hindu Lobby'—very much akin to the famed 'Jewish Lobby.' " (Keshavan had been a very good journalist before he became part of Ackerman's team; he died very young, at fifty-three.) The aspiration to become like AIPAC and to move India in the direction of Israel is strong among many of those who want to build this India (or Hindu) Lobby, geared as it is against Pakistan and without deference to the fact that the 120 million Indian Muslims are *Indians* too and not simply *Muslims.* A senior Democratic senator said in 2003, "All of us here are members of Likud now." If USINPAC succeeds, they'd perhaps say, "We're all members of the Hindu Right now."

AJC and AIPAC cultivated Indian officialdom. In 2003, AJC honored India's national security adviser, Brajesh Mishra, at its annual dinner, while it held another special dinner for India's home minister, L.K. Advani. Mishra told AJC that India was preparing to welcome Israel's leader, Ariel Sharon, to New Delhi in 2003. India's links with Israel were crucial for Israeli diplomacy: India is a core member of the Non-Aligned Movement, and its opinions continue to carry weight in the corridors of the United Nations. After 9/11, Israel courted India as a bulwark against criticism for its continued occupation of the Palestinian homeland, and the United States courted India to help isolate Iran. Such geopolitical chess moves had an impact on India's foreign ministry, whose own theory of world affairs had begun to change quite drastically. No more the nonaligned vision; now it was time for India to exert itself as a major player on the world stage. If the United States would adopt India as it had Israel, all would be well. But this view had detractors, not the least of whom was the Indian ambassador to the UN, Nirupam Sen. They had to be sidelined in favor of those who favored a more open pro-U.S. stance, and a more robust (that is to say, muscular, or military) foreign policy. John Bolton, Bush's man at the UN, called Sen an "unreformed Communist." To constrain his moves on behalf of an internationalist UN, the United States pressured the Indian government to send Sen a deputy (Ajai Malhotra) to "check his boss's antiquated instincts." In 2009, the government replaced Sen with Hardeep Singh Puri, who Ramesh Chandran, the head of the India-U.S. Forum of Parliamentarians, said is "much more modern" than Sen's "proclivity to cling to a leftist non-aligned mentality." In other words, Puri allowed the Indian government to be much more subservient to the U.S. narrative of world affairs.

The cost of the USINPAC-AIPAC approach to instability in places like South Asia is plain to see. After the Mumbai attacks of 2008, USINPAC held a "Washington *Chalo*" (Let's Go to Washington) lobbying event. They wanted to pressure the U.S. Congress to send a strong message to Islamabad, demanding that the Pakistani government turn over those whom India claimed were the masterminds of the attack on the Indian government. If this and other demands were not met, then the United States should reconsider its funding to Pakistan, and India would have all "options open," including military strikes. India and Pakistan have no extradition treaty. Making a demand that cannot be met is tantamount to a casus belli. The Washington *Chalo* event on January 27, 2009, was a damp squib. The "official" India Lobby privately scoffed at its amateurish display. The U.S. Congress was unimpressed.

What is remarkable about the Washington *Chalo* episode is the failure of groups such as USINPAC to fully grasp the dynamics of U.S. foreign policy. The linkage with Pakistan is integral to the War on Terror, and to the forward policy of the United States in the heart of Eurasia (which is to say, Afghanistan and northern Pakistan). Not only is this region essential to the overt mission to degrade al-Qaeda, but it is also central to the less remarked-upon bid by the Atlantic powers to exert NATO's reach into Asia (through Afghanistan) and into Africa (through Libya). Unlike the India Lobby, the government of Pakistan opened its active lobbying work in 2005, four years after 9/11 and many years after the Indian government had already established firm contacts on K Street and inside Congress. The Pakistanis hired Van Scoyoc Associates to push for more and more military contracts, including, as Junaid Rana points out, to lay "the basis of a partnership in the War on Terror that provided Pakistani military bases to the U.S. military and the guarantee of Pakistani sovereign airspace for U.S. drone attacks." Two years later, the government of Pakistan hired Cassidy & Associates, who had appointed Robin Raphael (former assistant secretary of state for South Asian affairs) to head its global affairs and trade consultancy group. Fortuitously for Pakistan, Raphael was appointed special representative to Pakistan and Afghanistan by the Obama administration in 2009, with charge over nonmilitary procurement. A few months before she moved from Cassidy to the Obama administration, Raphael oversaw Pakistan's efforts to secure five more years of funds. On April 2, 2009, Congress took up the Pakistan Enduring Assistance and Cooperation Enhancement (PEACE) Act of 2009, which promised Pakistan's government $3 billion for its military and $7.5 billion for humanitarian assistance, all over five years. The only condition related to India is impotent (Pakistan is asked "not to support any person or group that conducts violence, sabotage, or other activities meant to instill fear or terror in India"). Even the death of Osama bin Laden in May 2011, in the heart of Pakistan, had little impact on the funding to Pakistan: its centrality to the war in Afghanistan overrides all other considerations. USINPAC's politics appear naive in light of the general grammar of imperialism.

The "official" and "unofficial" India Lobbies share more than officialdom would care to publically recognize. Both are committed to the adoption of a right-wing point of view regarding conflict, where the political issues at stake are displaced in the service of security. Both share a remarkable complacency toward the context of violence, preferring the gated-community model of foreign affairs.

When historian Benedict Anderson wrote *Long-Distance Nationalism* (1994), he assumed that one of the crucial features of the extremism of the long-distance nationalists was that they did not have to live next to their enemies, and so could take intractable positions against them. But this is no longer the case as the dominant class in India begins to share some features of an extremism that cares little for the long-term consequences of its actions.

Remarkably, the Indian elections of April–May 2009 went by without the Mumbai attacks of 2008 as a major issue. The Indian Right and the establishment press whipped up the issue in late 2008, and it seemed that it would become a central theme as the campaign warmed up. But it didn't. The hundreds of millions of voters had other things on their minds. They refused to be diverted by worries about national security when their own insecurity was so much closer to home. The Indian farmers and factory workers worry about jobs and child care, food and health care, and about the well-being of their kin who patrol the stalemate in Kashmir and on the Indian borders. They have little room for cross-border truculence, the coin of the Indian Right. That bellicosity did not make an appearance during the election campaign is no evidence for its absence in the corridors of power, both in New Delhi and in Washington, D.C. The drawing rooms of the Indian elite and the lobby rooms of USINPAC resonate with the fantasies of domination mirrored in the Israeli Right and its Lobby.

Whether the BJP (the hard Right) or the Indian congress (the soft Right) are in power in New Delhi, their foreign policy will align itself with Tel Aviv and Washington. That will give a fillip to the fledgling Hindu Lobby, as yet an infant, waiting to be properly adopted.

THE MYTH OF THE "SAME EXTREMIST ENEMY"

USINPAC derived its analysis of world affairs from the toxic corridors of the right-wing and liberal imperialist think-tank world of Washington, D.C. (the intellectual gap between the American Enterprise Institute and the Brookings Institution's Saban Center is very narrow). USINPAC held two related briefs: to ensure that Indian Americans enjoy the same amount of political power they feel is held by the Jewish American community, and to deploy that power in the service of India, preferably in an Indo-U.S. alliance in the image of the U.S.-Israeli entente. The ideological unity between Israel, India, and the United States preached by USINPAC is this: to fight terrorism, namely "Islamic militancy," "Islamic fundamentalism," "Islamic extremism," or, in the previously quoted words of Congressman Lantos, "mindless, vicious, fanatic, Islamic terrorism." If we all agree that the enemy is Islamic terrorism, then the United States, Israel, and India have an urgent need for an axis.

Ann Schaffer, director of AJC's Belfer Center for American Pluralism, said of AJC assistance toward what would later become USINPAC, "We shared with them the Jewish approach to political activism. We want to give them the tools to further their political agenda." When asked about the common "political agenda" between Jewish Americans and Indian Americans, AJC Washington, D.C., regional director Charles Brooks said, "We're fighting the same extremist enemy. We want to help them become more effective in communicating their political will." Who is that global enemy? The proffered answer is Islamic extremism, but in some incarnations the enemy seems to be global Islam in general, or anyone who dares to challenge the supremacy of the current geopolitical dispensation (which goes by many names: free-market theorists call it globalization, whereas its critics call it imperialist globalization; the U.S. State Department describes it as the export of democracy, whereas its critics call it U.S. imperialism).

What is crucial to my analysis is that U.S. power does not target only global Islam as its enemy, even if al-Qaeda is its current assailant. The animus of U.S. imperialism is directed at all those forces that resist its hegemony, from the guerrillas in the Americas (FARC in Colombia, for example) to the North Korean regime. It was convenient for al-Qaeda, Gun Zionism, and Hindutva (Hinduness) to reduce U.S. policy to an enmity against Islam itself for their own ends (for al-Qaeda, to appeal to its radical Islamist base; for Gun Zionism and Hindutva, to purport that their state policy is identical to U.S. state policy).

The chairman of the board of trustees at USINPAC's origin, Jesal Amin, argued that the "terrorists" who target Israel are "interconnected with the Muslim terror groups operating elsewhere in the Middle East and South Asia." Amin, who is active in the Republican Party in a very prosperous and overwhelmingly white area of New Jersey, adopts the view—commonplace among Israeli conservatives—that any Muslim who acts against the interests of Israel, or India, is a terrorist, whether it is on behalf of the Palestinian Liberation Organization or Hamas, the Jammu and Kashmir Liberation Front or the Lashkar-e-Toiba. But he is not alone in this strategic reduction. Sue Ghosh Stricklett of USINPAC's Defense and Strategic Affairs Committee told a conservative publication, "We would like to see closer ties between the United States and India. Right now, India feels that Israel is a closer friend than the United States, and we would like to change that." In other words, it is valuable to reduce all forms of violence to "terrorism" in order to facilitate a geopolitical, economic alliance between India and the United States—regardless of the costs that others must bear for the prosperity that it will generate for a few.

Since the 1980s, one strand of the Indian American community has made it very clear that it lives within the worldview known as Hindutva. A political ideology within India that draws from European racist ideas of nationhood, Hindutva has taken the view, since its emergence in the 1920s, that Muslims do for it what Jews do for Nazism. In the United States such a view makes no sense, and it is translated into what I have called "Yankee Hindutva," where the Hindutva adherent relies upon liberal multiculturalism to give it space to develop its generally illiberal political identity that opposes not only Muslims, whether conservative or liberal, but also anything that it deems to be progressive and therefore a challenge to Hindutva. If there is any movement that cannot be held at bay, such as feminism, Hindutva attempts to accommodate it by attempting to glorify women who are independent and "traditional." Amin and Ghosh Stricklett's theory is not altogether common among upwardly mobile Indian Americans, mainly because

the middle class is motivated far more by convenience and upward mobility for its children than by ideology and sacrifice for
civilizational goals. Nevertheless, there are a few who adopt
the ideology emphatically. Twenty-one-year-old Nishkam
Gupta enlisted to fight in the 2003 U.S. war in Iraq as part of
his desire to "fight the larger war against terrorism, a war that
would directly benefit Hinduism and its cause." Kapil Sharma,
a consultant for the generally liberal IACPA, Gopal Raju's
shop, says, "We should be educated about each other's issues,
so we can talk about Kashmir and Palestine"—the two areas of
the world that, in the Indo-Israeli convergence, are now considered as parallels. The Hindutva–Gun Zionist framework has
leaked into the lives of those generally not predisposed to cruel
and macho nationalism.

There are several problems with the formulation offered by
people such as Amin, Stricklett, and AJC. They assume that
the Jihad International grows out of whole cloth from Islam,
from a few *suras* in the Koran or from the medieval history
of Arabia. There is a complete disregard for the history of the
Jihad International—how it came to be, its social forces, how
the United States and the Saudis, for instance, encouraged and
financed it as an alternative to the growth of republicanism and
communism. The Jihad International draws from the frustra-
tions of a generation who had been betrayed by the states that
claimed the mantle of anticolonial republicanism. Drawing
from the detritus of social thought in their home regions, these
groups remained largely anachronistic and without strength
until the United States gave them legitimacy and the Saudis
began to fund them, principally for the Afghan campaign
against the Soviets, but also in the war over Marxist South

Yemen. Gulf money and U.S. support oxygenated the harshest elements in these societies.

Groups like Hamas and the various factions in Kashmir certainly share ideological resources with the broader Jihad International, but they are also rooted in nationalist struggles. There is little doubt that Hamas and the various jihadi factions in Kashmir are a serious problem for the social development of their respective regions. Although Hamas does provide basic social services alongside its general policy of violence, this welfare is hardly to be considered valuable given the context within which it is offered. But to cast the Palestinians, Kashmiris, and others as the "extremist enemy" without a sense of how such factions attained prominence in their various struggles is to miss the hand of imperialism. Such a view also omits the many other Palestinian and Kashmiri organizations that revile the tactic of terror and the general social vision of Hamas and the Kashmiri jihadi groups, as well as the views of those who want to make a living and a life as much as change the world. To leave all this out erases the visions of social justice in such places, renders Islam itself into a one-dimensional tragedy, and casts out any hope for the progressive elements that strive against immense odds to turn the direction of the struggle around.

Furthermore, to render "terrorism" and "terrorists" as the enemy fails to distinguish between the tactics that a people use and the social and political conditions that generate their hostility: to defeat those who use terrorism, one has to understand and deal with the conditions that produce those who take to terror. All this is irrelevant to AIPAC and USINPAC.

The anxiety within the United States after 9/11 allowed

groups like USINPAC and AIPAC to make quick common cause on a myopic and toxic foundation. Half-baked assumptions about the terrorists (or "evildoers") generate fear but not analysis, and certainly not a strategy to deal with the problem. Ariel Sharon took advantage of the post-9/11 intellectual chaos in the United States to "change the facts on the ground" (as the Israeli high command likes to say) in both the West Bank and Gaza. His assaults in 2002–3 opened up a dynamic of Israeli aggression that continues to this day and is unabated by international condemnation. The Hindu Right, in power until 2004, wanted to mimic the Israeli strategy by bombing some madrassas and known terrorist camps in Pakistan, but neither the Indian military nor Indian public opinion countenanced such belligerence. (I remember a breezy chat with an Indian army man, long known to my family, who proudly told me how the midlevel officers like himself bristled during the 2001–2 mobilization along the India-Pakistan border after the attack on the Indian parliament; this show of force was called Operation Parakram, or Operation Strength.)

After the Mumbai attack in 2008, and after the U.S. raid on Osama bin Laden's compound in Abbottabad, the media in India tried to carry the standard for such a "surgical strike," joined breathlessly by the Hindu Right and the "realist" political theorists. The Hindu Right's parliamentary leader, L.K. Advani, said in 2008 referring to the Mumbai attacks, "This is not an attack. It is a war," and the government must take "whatever action [is] necessary"—in other words, a bombardment of Pakistan. The government held fast, pressured in large part by a very large public demonstration organized by hundreds of organizations in mid-December 2008 in Mumbai, and by the anxiety in Washington over the diversion of Pakistani troops from Pakistan's Afghan border to its Indian one. The Israeli road was ignored for the moment.

"Islamic militancy" and "terrorism" are code words that obfuscate the political landscape. The Israeli security establishment uses these terms to refer to any acts against their occupation of the Palestinian territories, whether it comes from the largely secular (even if corrupt) Fatah or the genuine fundamentalist (even if popular) Hamas. The Indian security establishment, and the hard Right, is equally brazen with these terms, given the use of them — in Kashmir, for example — to describe both the secular (Jammu and Kashmir Liberation Front) and communal (Hizb-e-Mujahideen) groups. Furthermore, the terror of the state and the terror of Hindutva or Gun Zionism are removed from the discussion. Sharad Gupta's exposé of a Bajrang Dal camp in Ayodhya introduces us to an Hindutva activist who tells him, "I am from the secret service of Bajrang Dal. Israel's Mossad is my inspiration. I can't tell you more."

The Bajrang Dal emerged out of the youth movement of the Hindu Right and took root against Muslims in the riots of 1992–93 and in the Dangs violence against Christian tribals in 1998–99. Even the Rashtriya Swayamsevak Singh (RSS), the brains of Hindutva's tentacles, had to disassociate itself from the terror of the Bajrang Dal (and its intelligence service, the so-called Desi Mossad). "All the riff-raff, the rejects of society. And the discards of the Sangh Parivar. These are the people who find refuge in the Bajrang Dal," said an RSS man. In their zealousness, the Dal members resemble the Israeli settlers who are often members of groups such as the Mafdal (National Religious Party), often of the fanatical Gush Emunim organization, and certainly operate as (in *Ha'aretz* journalist Doron Rosenblum's phrase) "Israeli settler warlords."

Prakash Sharma, national co-convener of the Dal, said his organization emulates Israel, where each citizen has to do mandatory physical training and military service. If Israel and India have a different geographical context for these measures, Sharma said, "India's [geographical situation] is even worse. Israel has threat only from outsiders while India faces threat from even those inhabiting it." The Indians who are Muslims will also be a threat to people like Sharma, just as the Arabs are always a dangerous feature of West Asia for Gun Zionism. This terror, the terror from Hindutva and Gun Zionism, is not to be tackled by the operational convergence of Shin Bet and RAW. What they will go after is just what the Gush Emunim and Bajrang Dal see as the problem; in this sense the intelligence agencies are as communal in their effect as the intentions of the most sectarian outfits. And these are all along the grain of their public relations firms in the United States, AIPAC, and USINPAC.

THE ISRAEL LOBBY

On July 16, 2003, AJC, AIPAC, and USINPAC held their first joint briefing. Congressman Frank Pallone, the New Jersey Democrat and former co-chair of the India Caucus, said, "One of the first things I would hear whenever I went around to the Indian American communities was how we can emulate the Jewish community, particularly how can we emulate AIPAC—in terms of their lobbying abilities, their grassroots abilities, their ability to organize the community politically."

Kumar Barve, the highest-elected Indian American and ma-jority leader in the Maryland House of Delegates, told the *Washington Post*, "I think Indian Americans see the American Jewish community as a yardstick against which to compare themselves. It's seen as the gold standard in terms of politi-cal activism." Reported Ajay Kuntamukkala, the president of the South Asian Bar Association of Washington, D.C., "A lot of folks in the Indian American community look at what Jews have done and try to model themselves after it."

In March 2006, respected political scientists Stephen Walt and John Mearsheimer wrote a treatise in the *London Review of Books* on the Israel Lobby (their essay was published as a bestselling book the following year). Walt and Mearsheimer catalogued both the institutional heft of the Lobby and its re-markable influence across the spectrum of U.S. government and public opinion. At the heart of the Lobby sits AIPAC, but its true genius is that it lies at the center of almost a hundred pro-Israel groups and coordinates their donations. These myr-iad political action groups "draw money from Jewish donors and operate under obscure-sounding names [and] are operated by AIPAC officials or people who hold seats on AIPAC's two major policymaking bodies." Money lubricates the U.S. po-litical system, and AIPAC has been able to strategically use its funds to gain the support of a slew of elected representatives. In terms of its operational mechanisms, Walt and Mearsheimer argue, "the Israel Lobby is no different from the farm lobby, steel or textile workers' unions, or other ethnic lobbies. There is nothing improper about American Jews and their Christian allies attempting to sway U.S. policy: the Lobby's activities are not a conspiracy of the sort depicted in tracts like the *Protocols of the Elders of Zion.*" Instead, the Israel Lobby is a special-interest public relations ensemble that is wedded to the idea that Israel's needs must be facilitated by U.S. power.

When Charles Brooks of AJC says, "We're fighting the same extremist enemy," the question to ask is, Who is included in "we"? For Walt and Mearsheimer, the Israel Lobby is not the property of Jewish Americans. Rather, many Jewish Americans set themselves apart from this Lobby, with 36 percent telling a 2004 survey that they were not overly emotionally linked to Israel. AJC and AIPAC do not speak for all Jews in the United States, for the mythical "Jewish American community." The community is fractured in its support for various political parties and agendas in Israel, as well as on the importance of being behind Israel at all (the founding of J-Street in 2008 to temper the AIPAC and AJC dominance of the debate is important to recall). In my two decades in the United States, I have worked alongside American Jewish comrades in almost all the struggles with which I have been involved (from the antiapartheid movement, to the El Salvador solidarity work, to labor struggles, to antiwar work, to work against the destruction of the U.S. welfare net). The river of radicalism runs deeply through the world of American Jewry. This tradition is well analyzed by the philosopher Judith Butler in the August 21, 2003, issue of the *London Review of Books*:

> The ethical framework within which most progressive Jews operate takes the form of the following question: will we be silent (and thereby collaborate with illegitimately violent power), or will we make our voices heard (and be counted among those who did what they could

to stop that violence), even if speaking poses a risk? The current Jewish critique of Israel is often portrayed as insensitive to Jewish suffering, past as well as present, yet its ethic is based on the experience of suffering, in order that suffering might stop.

The strand of anti-Zionist politics among American Jews draws strength from the litany of anti-Zionist organizations within Israel itself. Those who dissent from Israeli state policy are, however, part of a weakened tradition that has been unable to combat the overwhelming but incorrect notion that any criticism of Israel is anti-Semitic. In both Israel and the United States, there is a consensus that tends to the Gun Zionism view.

If the Israel Lobby is not the public relations firm for Jewish Americans, then what is it? Certainly it speaks for many Jewish Americans, who do have a strong emotional allegiance to the state of Israel. This strand of opinion was limited until the 1967 war, before which few Jewish Americans identified themselves with Israel. In his 1957 survey of Jewish American attitudes, the sociologist Nathan Glazer found that Israel "had remarkably slight effects on the inner life of American Jewry." Only one in twenty American Jews traveled to Israel before June 1967, and intellectuals at an AJC symposium on Jewish identity held a few months before the war barely considered Israel in their comments. After the war, when Israel became a crucial player in U.S. strategy, Israel became, according to Norman Podhoretz, editor of the neoconservative *Commentary*, "the religion of the American Jews," at least of the mainstream Zionist organizations.

Alongside sections of the Jewish American community that is wedded to AIPAC are evangelical Christians (organized into Christians United for Israel) who have their own peculiar reason to support Israel: they believe in the theory of dispensationalism, with the current dispensation (Grace) soon to give way to the final dispensation (Rapture), and to speed this up the Jews need to be in control of Israel, shepherd the building of the Second Temple, and then be damned. Rabbi David Rosen says of this view, "This poses a paradoxical problem — that very often those who love Israel don't really love Judaism," or, he might have added, Jews. Jerry Falwell, the evangelical preacher, was often given to deeply anti-Semitic statements about Jews (in 1980 he said, "A few of you don't like Jews and I know why. He can make more money accidentally than you can make on purpose"). Falwell was a ferocious supporter of Israel as a lever to the Rapture: "The Jews are returning to their land of unbelief. They are spiritually blind and desperately in need of their Messiah and Savior. Yet they are God's people, and in the world today Bible-believing Christians are the best friends the nation of Israel has." When the Anti-Defamation League took evangelicals to task for statements such as Falwell's, and Pat Robertson's *The New World Order* (1994), a prehistoric racist screed, leading neoconservatives such as Irving Kristol, Midge Decter, and Gertrude Himmelfarb took out an advertisement in the *New York Times*, saying, "On the survival of Israel, the Jews have no more stalwart friends than evangelical Christians." Rabbi Marc Tanenbaum of AJC agreed, "The evangelical community is the largest and fastest-growing bloc of pro-Jewish sentiment in this country." What he meant was pro-Israel, for they are hardly pro-Jewish.

Walt and Mearsheimer add another dimension to the concept of the Israel Lobby. It is not simply a lobby that represents various domestic constituencies (evangelical Christians, sections of the Jewish American population). It is also the Washington, D.C., arm of the Israeli government. In 2003, Sharon told a Washington, D.C., gathering, "People ask me how they can help Israel. I tell them: 'Help AIPAC.' " Israel also hires its own lobbyists, and it has close affiliations with various think tanks that trend toward the neoconservative and Gun Zionist lines, such as the Washington Institute for Near East Policy and the Jewish Institute for National Security Affairs, not to speak of the putatively neutral groups such as the Saban Center for Middle East Policy (at the Brookings Institution). Alongside all these are the less subtle parts of the Lobby, such as the arms industry, the oil industry, and others who favor a strong Israel in a turbulent Middle East. It is fortuitous for AIPAC that its views align with the neoconservative elements that dominate the Middle East policy establishment in Washington, and that its interests are currently aligned with those of corporations that have remarkable amounts of influence in the U.S. political system.

The U.S. Congress stands united behind Israel. Any dissension is met with the reproach of anti-Semitism. If this is the work of the Israel Lobby, then it has achieved a remarkable feat: a totally bipartisan Congress with little opposition to its general goals. When AIPAC and AJC go to Washington now, they meet receptive, even eager ears. The lobbyists did not alone create the conditions for Israel's elevation. U.S. foreign policy does the work for them.

No such magnificent condition exists for India. The U.S.

nexus with Pakistan means that New Delhi can never have as cozy a relationship with Washington as Tel Aviv enjoys. Only a measured approach to the entire region, with a plan for a settlement of the border dispute and confidence between the two nuclear powers, is sensible. Anything else will make India subservient to Washington and help to keep an unstable neighborhood volatile.

THE MYTH OF THE MODEL MINORITY

AIPAC, whatever its role in the Israel Lobby, has certainly come to play a crucial role in the Jewish American community. As Esther Kaplan of Jews for Ethnic and Racial Justice said on her radio show *Beyond the Pale* in 2002, groups like AIPAC and AJC leverage their closeness to U.S. power to claim the mantle of the Jewish American mainstream for themselves. Even if AIPAC does not represent the majority or the plurality of American Jews, it claims to be representative and attempts to fulfill its claim. AIPAC's Zionism and its claim to be the representative of Jewish America mean that the community appears to be far more conservative than it perhaps is. Do all Jewish Americans align with the views of AIPAC and AJC, or indeed with Gun Zionism's current standard, Israeli prime minister Binyamin Netanyahu? No. What is more important is the way immigrant or ethnic organizations pose as representatives of the power structure regardless of their actual depth in their community.

Immigrants in the United States have an idiosyncratic relationship to the world of politics. Despite the racist divisions in our civil society, there is no referendum or election process for the leader of each of the social communities. So how does "ethnic leadership" emerge? There are some organic processes—for example, the efforts of community organizations that not only represent the community but also constitute and reproduce it. Among Indian Americans, regional and linguistic groups (Gujarat Samaj, Tamil Sangam) are one example, and so are the national professional groups (Asian American Hotel Owners Association, American Association of Physicians of Indian Origin). Then there are those groups that work within the community to transform practices undesirable to some or to fashion a new desi social culture (women's rights groups, gay and lesbian groups, workers' rights groups). The people who could be leaders are those who put their energy into these organizations and into the reproduction of the desi community through the festivals and protests, the gatherings for joy and justice. But, as with most post-1965 immigrant groups, the leaders of these organizations are not the most visible representatives of the community in the realm of electoral politics.

It takes little to set up a political shop: the name of an organization, a patron among one or the other party or lobby group, fancy-looking letterhead, a fairly dynamic leader, and preferably a photograph or two of this leader with an important politician from one of the two major parties and/or an important politician from the homeland. The picture with the politician is almost sufficient to indicate that our fearless leader has cachet in the world of Washington, and his or her back door to power allows him or her to play a disproportionate role as the "representative" of the immigrant community before the established power structure. These figures become brokers for the major parties as they try to reach out to the immigrant communities for votes, and they become symbolic figureheads for the community itself. USINPAC is one such immigrant entity.

AIPAC and the Indian American high-profile groups not only use their closeness to U.S. power; they also wield the myth of the model minority to capture the hearts and minds of their constituency and to make a broader appeal in a country wedded to antiblack racism. The Indian American community is rent with divisions, those of class and region, caste and religion, and of course of political affiliation. Whatever the disagreements over politics in the subcontinent, the general tenor of the Indian American community is to lean toward liberalism (and in its organized form, the Democratic Party). While there are no good survey data on Indian American social and political attitudes, my own reading of the ethnographic literature and my own political involvement in the community suggest that the bulk of desis are against immigration controls and the death penalty, for the right of a woman to control her own body (or at least against the ban on abortion), for better wages for working people, for better care for the elderly, and for health insurance coverage. Among second-generation desis the trend of liberalism runs deeper. With the fear of terror, manipulations by groups like USINPAC, and the consolidation of professional success for a sizable section of the community, there has been over the years a perceptible turn to conservatism.

One of those who moved to the Republican Party was Jesal Amin, the founder of what would become USINPAC. Amin, onetime leader of the Indian Business Association of New Jersey and its local branch of the Asian American Retailers Association, has also run for public office on the Republican Party line. He has not had much success. Amin was instrumental in bringing AIPAC and AJC to help form the Hindu Lobby. What brought Amin to the attention of the AIPAC and others was his work with Jewish American groups against hate crimes in New Jersey. He holds firmly to the view that the terrorists who operate in India are linked to those that operate in Israel. But his insistence on the links between Jewish Americans and Indian Americans did not come from this kind of geopolitical vision—rather, from even more mundane ideological reasons: the view that both Jews and Indians are model minorities in the United States. "We have made the American dream come true," he said in 2002. "Many Indians are professional. One of the reasons for working together with the Jewish community is that we are so similar in terms of education, and from an economic point of view." The late Tom Lantos, Democrat from California and an immigrant from Hungary, went over the top: "There is a natural symbiotic relationship between the Indian community and the Jewish community," he said. "It begins with respect for life. There is no community for whom the sacredness of life is as prominent in its philosophy than the Indian community and we Jews—when we drink, we say '*Rafiat*,' which means life." On a more practical level, he said, "There is a profound relationship in our passionate commitment to education. We have a passionate commitment to respect for others, for the rule of law, and for democracy, and lately, we've been brought together by our joint fight against mindless, vicious, fanatic Islamic terrorism."

How does one even begin to analyze these banal generalities? Do all Jews and Indians have a passionate respect for others? Even those Indians (perhaps he means Hindus) who killed innocent people in Gujarat in 2002, or those Jews (as Israeli citizens) who killed the Palestinians of Jenin in 2002? Is the assumption that a people have a culture that is singular not itself a species of racialist thinking that we must abhor? These are some basic questions that are worth posing. When Congressman Lantos says that Jews and Indians are passionate about education, when Amin says that Jews and Indians are similar in terms of education, do they mean that there are people in the world who are not interested or invested in education, who would prefer illiteracy? What does it mean to say that some people are favored, are chosen, if not to also say that there are others who are misbegotten? This kind of statement has a long history, going back at least to Sardar Panikkar (quoted at the start of this chapter), and into the gutter of the Hindu Right. In a 1967 issue of *The Organiser*, the RSS's magazine, Chitragupta wrote frankly about the implications of these sorts of statements:

Why did the Israelis and we in our struggle against Pakistan fare better than the Pakistanis and the Arabs? It is simply a question of the mind behind the machine but dominating and using it instead of being used by it. The Islamic world is not destitute of genius, or ability, but it has not been given a dog's chance because it is under the benumbing control of a rigid theology and petrified dogma. The Jew and the Hindu have been eclectic without ceasing to be Hindus or Jews because of their devotion to the pursuit of truth without blinders, their readiness to see other points of view than their own and willingness to live and let live.

The clichés in Chitragupta's essay bumble out of the mouths of respected American intellectuals and politicians, people who might avoid saying the sentence about the "dog's chance," but might think it anyway. The statement about the connection between Jews and Hindus is commonplace between Ackerman and Barve, both liberal Democrats. There is no awkwardness about that half of the argument, since they suppress the other part (about Islam), leaving it unsaid so that it speaks even louder in the silence of the mind.

In 1965, after a century of struggle and sacrifice, the movement for civil rights won an impressive victory. The United States adopted a bill that gave every citizen formal equality before the law, thereby annulling the premise of Jim Crow segregation. The victory was immense but partial. It demolished formal equality, but it did not say anything about the everyday inequality that had been structured into every aspect of social life. As one of the architects of the classical civil rights movement, Bayard Rustin, put it, "The very decade which has witnessed the decline of legal Jim Crow has also seen the rise of de facto segregation in our most fundamental socioeconomic institutions." The movement against racism was interested in much greater freedoms than simply the right to vote, one of which was the demand for reparations or a transfer of capital stolen from labor that had not been paid for centuries. The famous 1963 March on Washington was called, for instance, the March on Washington for Civil Rights and Jobs. The reforms of the United States did not address this latter crucial demand. When the civil rights movement transmuted into the Black Power movement, the U.S. government and sections of its intelligentsia revised their older racist notions and practices for what has been called the New Racism of our epoch. That is, the state must now treat everyone equal before the law, economic demands are left outside the purview of the question of race, and certain previously oppressed people (such as Jews and Asians) can obtain some privileges, while those who are the descendants of enslaved people are left penniless, hopeless, and therefore one step from criminality. Outspoken blacks would be criticized for their lack of solicitude.

When the mainly black community of Watts, Los Angeles, rose in rebellion in 1965, the United States appeared incensed and shocked. In 1966 the mainstream periodical *U.S. News & World Report* published one of the first positive articles about Asians. Once reviled as the Yellow Peril, Chinese Americans, the article said, believed in "the old idea that people should depend on their own efforts—not a welfare check—in order to reach America's 'promised land.'" This autonomous effort, the magazine noted, came at "a time when it is being proposed that hundreds of billions of dollars be spent to uplift Negroes and other minorities." That same year, Irving Kristol asked in the *New York Times Magazine*, "Can the Negro be expected to follow the path of previous immigrant groups [Jews and Italians] or is his a special, 'pathological' case?" What is being said is this: the Asians work hard without complaint, and so should the blacks; the Jews work hard, and so should the blacks. This erases the hard work and low pay endured by African Americans, most of whom, because of the incomplete dismantling of the Jim Crow structure, did not have access to any other kind of work. Kristol wrote, "The real tragedy of the American Negro today is not that he is poor, or black, but that he is a latecomer—he confronts a settled and highly organized society whose assimilatory powers have markedly declined over the past decades." But Africans had been brought to the Americas long before Jews and Italians, so that when Kristol says "latecomers," he must mean to the feast of capital, since most blacks worked to produce the bounty that was divided among some whites in an earlier time. By this logic, blacks are blamed for the failures of American history.

Jews, like Asians, long reviled by the U.S. power structure, became acceptable, as scholar Karen Brodkin showed in *How Jews Became White Folks*, only in the late 1960s, as beneficiaries of the New Racism and of the military victory of Israel in 1967. The geography of Jewish migration and the sociology of Jewish achievement became irrelevant to the narrative of Jewish success. There is no consideration of the trials of the nineteenth-century Jewish working class that helped fight to build the U.S. labor movement and the various social movements of the early part of the century, nor is there an acknowledgment of the large numbers of Jewish Americans who live outside the charmed circle of plutocratic success enjoyed by a celebrated few. According to the Metropolitan Council on Jewish Poverty, in 2002 there were 430,000 poor and near-poor Jewish Americans in New York City alone (out of a total population of about 1.97 million). Their lives are not available inside the sterotype.

The Indians that came to the United States because of the 1965 immigration reforms also benefited from this New Racism: before these laws we were regarded as blacks, but after them we could aspire to whiteness. Twenty-five percent of Indian Americans put themselves down as "white" in the 1990 Census (in her 2001 voter registration card, South Carolina governor Nikki Haley put herself down as "white" as well; she was born Nimrata Randhawa in South Carolina to Sikh parents, but washed that away).

Arriving in the United States in droves between the mid-1960s and the early 1980s, Indian Americans rose in the ranks of their professions and made very high salaries. But their attainments were not caused by natural or cultural selection, as I showed in *The Karma of Brown Folk*. If this were the case, the one billion Indians in India would all be doctors and nurses, engineers and scientists. Rather, it was the result of state selection, whereby the United States, through the special skills provision in the 1965 Immigration Act, fundamentally configured the demography of Indian America. Between 1965 and 1977, 83 percent of the migrants came with advanced degrees. State selection, not the natural selection of millennia, brought highly qualified desis to the United States. Those who hold power in the United States use the anomalous demographic of professional desis to show that we succeed while other minorities fail, that we succeed because we work hard, while they fail because they are either incapable or lazy. The history of why we succeed is lost in this simple story. And thanks to its refusal of history, the stereotype tends to confirm antiblack racism.

Why should Jewish Americans and Indian Americans get together? Because they are human beings, because some may share ideological positions, because a few may share personal tastes. These are less offensive ways to create solidarity than to jointly bear the burden of stereotyped traditions (peaceful people, etc.) or to leverage our friendship on the backs of blacks. The latter, as the novelist Toni Morrison wrote, is a typical, homespun strategy for advancement in the United States. The immigrant, she noted, must participate "freely in this most enduring and efficient rite of passage into American culture: negative appraisals of the native-born black population. Only when the lesson of racial estrangement is learned is assimilation complete. Whatever the lived experience of immigrants with African Americans—pleasant, beneficial, or bruising—the rhetorical experience renders blacks as noncitizens, already discredited outlaws." Jews and Indians, both of whom live in a racist polity, take shelter in the false praises of their greatness. Far better to be seen as good than evil, but at what social cost do a people want acclaim? Who pays for desis to be the "model minority"?

The high-profile organizations leverage their proximity to power and their ideology of the model minority to attract large numbers of desis to their ranks, or to the tug of their beliefs. The cost of this, however, is to leave desis outside the major struggles for social justice that is the best thing about America.

STRANGE BEDFELLOWS

Politics does make strange bedfellows. Three decades ago, the alliance between Indian American and Jewish American groups would have seemed impossible. For one, the Indian government was not openly in favor of the Israeli state—a mark against it, from AIPAC's point of view. When it declined to issue visas to Israeli delegations, particularly to sports teams, the Indian government earned the ire of U.S.-based Jewish organizations. In 1987, the Anti-Defamation League, for instance, wrote, "It is time for the international community to let India know that unless it ceases to inject its anti-Israel policies into events aimed at furthering the spirit of international cooperation, it will be forced to forfeit its frequent role as host nation." The alliance between Indian American and Jewish American mainstream organizations plainly has little to do with "cultural values" but a lot to do with the geopolitical alliance between India and Israel. When it comes to Israel, AJC and AIPAC will make alliances with anyone who, for whatever reason, is willing to defend the right of Gun Zionism to make mayhem in West Asia. Jason F. Isaacson, director of government and international affairs of AJC, told the press, "All three countries [India, Israel, and the United States] really need to stick together not only because of the common threats of terrorism but because of commonalities and values, and that is the message we are going to convey." These common values are not shared by all Indians, Israelis, and Americans in the same way: they may want to do different things when faced with specific forms of terror that come from very particular social forces.

What does this have to say about race in post-9/11 America? As the "Muslim" increasingly bears the mark of Cain, it opens up immense opportunities for middle-class people of color to demonstrate their patriotism in anti-Islamic terms. For the contingent working class, such an opportunity is not afforded. Those who are of color in this class fragment bear the brunt of systemic racism, and their patriotism is easily eclipsed by their imputed immorality and criminality. Those who are not prone to functional unemployment or contingent status and are of color as a block are mainly immigrants like those from South Asia. Race, since 9/11, has not included desis as victims of racial profiling and thereby has expanded the targets for state racism. It has instead fashioned a complex racial landscape where groups jockey to get out from under the racist gaze of society and the racist policies of the state. For such immigrants, the post-9/11 scenario offers few decent options: either claim solidarity with a people who have become the image of international terrorism, or pledge your patriotism through abjuration of any cultural links with Islam or Muslims, indeed to make the "Muslim" your enemy. If the "Muslim" becomes your enemy, and if you have the cultural capital to fly above the quicksand of the contingent class, then you have the opportunity to be "American."

5

Compulsions of Ethnicity

Sonal Shah, *India Abroad* Person of the Year, 2003.
Bobby Jindal, *India Abroad* Person of the Year, 2005.
Indra Noori, *India Abroad* Person of the Year, 2006.
Nikki Haley, *India Abroad* Person of the Year, 2010.

You know you've assimilated when one of your own is charged with white-collar crime. The trial of Galleon's CEO Raj Rajaratnam was the final straw. The home base of South Asian America is now secure: we too can be crooks. Rajaratnam was charged with insider trading, the classic crime of post-1981 America. One of his accomplices is Rajat Gupta, one of the great gurus at McKinsey and then on the board of Goldman Sachs, who is worth millions of dollars. In the stratosphere of finance capital, $1 million is not enough. All the pinstripes want to add another zero to their portfolios. Greed is as important as dignity.

An even clearer sign of our political arrival is when a politician who shares ancestry with an immigrant community runs for and wins office without any fealty to or even obligation to that community. Louisiana governor Bobby Jindal is the classic case, but so too is South Carolina governor Nikki Haley and, in a different way, White House insider Sonal Shah. These are politicians who are not accountable to their community but nonetheless often stand in for it. And because they stand in for it, there is a sentiment among many of us that despite their views, they must be defended. Those are the compulsions of ethnicity.

By the compulsions of ethnicity, the *community* has to be supportive of the politician or the crook (in some cases the same person). Their standing reflects on the community even as they have no organic link to it.

OBAMA AND THE END OF MULTICULTURALISM

Multiculturalism in the United States of America ended on the night of November 4, 2008. When Barack Obama walked onto the stage at Grant Park and accepted the mantle of the presidency of the United States, an epoch that opened up in the 1980s came to an end. No longer could the argument be made that high office in the public and private sectors wasn't open to those who had suffered the modern stigma of being "lesser." All branches of the higher offices have welcomed people of African, Asian, or Latin American descent: Thurgood Marshall and Sonia Sotomayor have been Justices of the U.S. Supreme Court, General Colin Powell has been the head of the Joint Chiefs of Staff, and many, many people of color have been chief executive officers of Fortune 500 firms. The day of the glass ceiling is now over. Multiculturalism promised to end it, and it did. Obama is president, Sotomayor interprets the laws, and Pepsi's Indra Noori sells you what you need.

Multiculturalism is over, but not racism. This is certainly not a postracist moment, even as it is indeed a postmulticultural one. Before he won the presidential election, Obama told journalist Gwen Ifill for her 2009 book *The Breakthrough*, "Race is a factor in this society. The legacy of Jim Crow and slavery has not gone away. It is not an accident that African Americans experience high crime rates, are poor, and have less wealth. It is a direct result of our racial history. We have never fully come to grips with that history." Little is made of this remarkable statement. Obama, Deval Patrick (governor of Massachusetts), Cory Booker (mayor of Newark), and others tell us that they are fully aware of the new advantages of the post–Jim Crow era, but they are not blind to the glaring inequities and injustices that persevere in our society. Where they appear to be blindsided is in their analysis of what is possible in this new era, on how to engender an antiracist politics in the new grammar of the post–civil rights era. The debate on "postracism" misses its mark. The point isn't whether the United States is in a postracist phase or not, but that while racism has morphed over the past thirty years, multiculturalism has enabled some people to advance, to enjoy the fruits of the American dream at the same time as the system was drastically transformed to curtail this dream from the majority of the population.

Alice's Dream

Alice Hicks had two pictures on the wall in her living room: portraits of John F. Kennedy and Martin Luther King Jr. When I first went to her home in the early 1990s, it was as a community organizer coming to make contact with a veteran in the struggles for justice in Providence, Rhode Island. Alice was one of the key people of the DARE (Direct Action for Rights and Equality) community. DARE could not have begun in 1986 without the support of community stalwarts like Alice. She was a rock, leading many fights in her neighborhood. People worked, but they didn't seem to make enough to pay for their basic needs (including heat and food). A garbage incinerator spewed toxins into the air as absentee landlords abandoned properties that had become garbage lots. And, to top it all, the police were unnecessarily aggressive against the young people who struggled to find dignity as they came of age. I remember Alice, even as she struggled with her own health, coming to meetings, sitting down, and quietly fulminating about problems, or being on the street at a press conference or demonstration. She was a pillar of strength.

Each time I went to pick her up for a meeting, and as I waited for her to get her things or to get me something to drink (which was part of her obligatory kindness), I stared at the portraits. One day, casually, I asked her why she had a picture of JFK on the wall. I could understand the King picture, but not that of a man who had not given King and his movement the kind of support necessary. And besides, I said, it was LBJ who pushed Congress to pass the Civil Rights and Voting Rights Acts. She smiled at me, ready to indulge my impertinence. "Of course President Johnson did those things. And those acts were important. But were they enough? What did they get us? This . . ." Her weak arms opened expansively to encompass not her living room but her neighborhood, her world. "President

Johnson gave us something. I accept that. But it was Dr. King and President Kennedy who allowed us to dream. President Johnson's real gift was not even a pale shadow of those dreams."

I didn't understand the enormity of what Alice told me that morning until years later. Politically it was clear that the civil rights struggle's major legislative victories were both enormously important and far too limited. Almost two hundred years after the birth of the United States, people of African ancestry were able to claim the franchise unhindered by all kinds of legal blocks and to claim the right to social and political dignity. *After* President Johnson signed both the Civil Rights Act (1964) and the Voting Rights Act (1965), Dr. King took the pulpit of the Ebenezer Baptist Church in Atlanta, Georgia (July 4, 1965), to remind his congregation of his dream from the March on Washington (1963). "My dream," he said now, "has often turned into a nightmare." Brave civil rights workers have been shot, he recounted, and the condition of black life has deteriorated, so that there are many "Harlems of our nation." "I've seen my dream shattered as I've walked the streets of Chicago and seen Negroes, young men and women, with a sense of utter hopelessness because they can't find any jobs. And they see life as a long and desolate corridor with no exit signs. And not only Negroes at this point. I've seen my dream shattered because I've been through Appalachia, and I've seen my white brothers along with Negroes living in poverty." But this had not killed his dream entirely. "I still have a dream," he preached, "that one day all of God's children will have food and clothing and material well-being for their bodies, culture and education for their minds, and freedom for their spirits." I read this sermon, called "The American Dream," in 1998, about five years after that morning with Alice. She prepared me for it, to see the 1964–65 laws both as a culmination of a struggle and as the opening of a new struggle. A portrait of President Johnson might have meant that the story had ended with the laws. But the presence of the portraits of President Kennedy and Dr. King indicated that the unfinished dream was more powerful than the small victories that come on the way.

Thirty Years Too Late

You give me second-class houses,
and second-class schools.
Do you think all colored folks
Are just second-class fools?

—Nina Simone/Langston Hughes, 1966

The tragedy of the age of integration (1954 onward) is that it overlapped with the demise of the social-wage state and the rise of the neoliberal social order. The victory of this movement came thirty years too late. Just when the United States agreed to remove the discriminatory barriers that restricted nonwhites' access to public goods, the form of the state changed. Privatization and the assault of the state's provision of social welfare (in the most expansive sense) meant that it was not capable of providing the public goods to the newly enfranchised citizens. You win, but the prize is hollow.

The civil rights movement fought for the widest provision of dignity: for the freedom to eat and dream, to study and work, to relax and pray. Human needs squashed by enslavement and by the rigid Jim Crow codes asserted themselves in the remarkable mass social movement that emerged after World War II and catapulted toward victory after the Supreme Court's 1954 verdict in *Brown v. Board of Education* and the 1955 Montgomery bus boycott. The Court gave sanction from above while the boycott gave hope from below.

From the New Deal of the 1930s to the Great Society of the 1960s, the United States entered the world of social commerce and interaction with an agenda to benefit people across the lines of class. Progressive movements in the nineteenth century had pushed against governmental institutions that had given themselves over to the needs of business—in particular, the very large monopoly firms and their owners. Populists and progressives, socialists and abolitionists, trade unionists and farmers all demanded more from the state to which they paid their taxes. All they got was sanctimonious speeches and the baton. Only when the economy cracked and the ruling elites had no other means to save their economic system did one or two moderate ideas come to the surface. Pushed by the unemployment councils and the gaunt faces of the starving peasantry, the state in the 1930s finally provided relief and reconstruction for the life-world of the workers. The concept that united the many social programs of this period was the social wage. The social wage is that amount of deferred wages that goes toward the creation of various publicly available goods, such as transportation, health services, schools, parks, postal delivery, public safety, and so forth. The beautiful concept of the social wage implies that public services are available to all, regardless of income and social standing, even as they are paid for by a progressive tax scheme.

A universal concept in the world of abstract ideas, the social wage came into being in this period in much less elevated ways. The Depression hit most people very hard, even those who had little to lose before the collapse of the economy (as Langston Hughes put it, "The Depression brought everybody down a peg or two. And the Negro had but few pegs to fall"). The Roosevelt administration put substantial resources toward relief for the population, including for African Americans (by 1935, African Americans comprised 20 percent of those on relief, even as African Americans made up only 10 percent of the population). Writing in his major study on discrimination in the United States, the sociologist Gunnar Myrdal noted, "For almost the first time in the history of the nation the state has done something substantial in a social way without excluding the Negro." Relief came as charity, though not as the means for advancement. The state entered the housing market to send African Americans into public housing projects and not to the new middle-class towns. Segregation, a major target of the civil rights movement, was reinforced. A house is not just a place to live, but also equity to borrow against. So when whites got federal loans to buy homes, they were also given a down payment in the American dream—to send their kids to college, to buy a car, to advance themselves up the greasy pole of the organizational society. African Americans and other people of color did not get these benefits, sent, as they were, to penniless neighborhoods or public housing, neither of which drew the commercial banks with their checkbooks. Public space and public services for those of color had been severely compromised.

If the social wage did not fully take hold of the lives of African Americans and other people of color (Latinos, Asians, Native Americans), it also didn't fully do what was necessary for all women either. The domain of "women's work" in general was not taken in hand by the state. When women's organizations and women trade unionists voiced demands for public child care, as an example, they were turned aside. White women did, however, benefit from the perquisites of the social wage, from the parks and schools, transportation networks, and other services.

Those whom the state deemed to be white lived a charmed life. Federal dollars came to them as housing loans in subdivisions blessed with state-sponsored water and sewer lines, and these suburbs existed at the edges of cities, linked to them with state-built freeways on which the new suburbanites drove their mortgaged cars powered by state-subsidized gasoline. This ensemble is what historian George Lipsitz calls the "possessive investment in whiteness." The illusion of the free market masked the immense government subvention.

The civil rights movement emerges in the 1950s partly as a demand for the breakdown of the barriers to the full enjoyment of the social wage. Three million African Americans and half a million Latinos (as well as considerable numbers of Asian Americans and Native Americans) fought in World War II. They traveled far from the narrow confines of Jim Crow oppression, enjoying the fresh air of the other continents where they came to terms with the fact that they could die for their country but weren't allowed to live in it. During the war as well, large numbers of African Americans migrated to the burgeoning cities of the South as well as the North. Here they lived in close quarters with each other as well as worked in the expanding industrial sector. Joining unions allowed them to have the practical experience of being organized and a corporeal sense of the power this involved. By 1945, one and a half million African Americans were union members. In California and Texas, Latinos moved against the recalcitrant Anglo-dominated political and economic system through such venues as the American G.I. Forum and the Community Service Organization (both founded in 1948). History's small voices became a mighty scream against a system run on the labor and disenfranchisement of people of color.

Integration didn't just mean that everyone should sit at the same lunch counter or study in the same classroom (you don't have to live next to me, just give me my equality). It also meant that people, regardless of their place in society, should have access to the social wage. No more redlining to restrict people of color from buying houses that they can afford with loans guaranteed by the federal government. No more preventing young students of color from resources given to other students, thereby providing them with opportunities to leverage their intelligence for economic betterment. Access to public space and to state-sponsored social advantages comprised the legal right to the social wage.

The Civil Rights Act allowed people of color to benefit from the social wage (transportation, education, etc.) and social insurance (Social Security, welfare, etc.). It was in and through the New Deal state that people of color would claim their deferred or indirect wages. The state stood before them as the bulwark against racism and the bank for their economic dreams. Affirmative action schemes in the public sector strengthened this impression, and before long, the largest union for African Americans, for example, became AFSCME, the American Federation of State, County, and Municipal Employees.

From the mid-1960s on, the character of the United States went through a complete overhaul. The New Deal era "social wage state" slowly withered as the neoliberal era "corporate wage state" took its place. No longer would the state intervene against inequality and for justice, even in the halfhearted way it did. Now the state would conduct itself as the exemplar of restraint, pushing for discipline in the money markets and on the streets, reining in social spending and social disorder. Corporate power over the state increased at the expense of democracy, a shift that had drastic results for those communities who had only just been allowed into the ambit of the social wage and equality. In this sense, the victory of the civil rights movement was thirty years too late. When it came, the Bank of Justice was broke.

Tragic Enigma

The legal and electoral gains of the civil rights movement have been significant but limited, particularly as the state form changed and the promises of economic mobility began to sour. The ambit of antiracism, as far as the establishment was concerned, narrowed to the legal, political, and cultural domain. It was this third, as multiculturalism, that grew legs in the 1980s. Both Barack Obama and I were in college in the 1980s. Our world was wrapped around thinking of the massive social changes and experimenting with life in a post–Jim Crow world. "We smoked cigarettes," he writes in *Dreams of My Father*, "and wore leather jackets. At night, in the dorms, we discussed neocolonialism, Frantz Fanon, Eurocentrism, and patriarchy. When we ground out our cigarettes in the hallway carpet or set our stereos so loud that the walls began to shake, we were resisting bourgeois society's stifling constraints. We weren't indifferent or careless or insecure. We were alienated." It was the task of multiculturalism to embed us in the social mores, to bring us out of our alienation.

Being in college during the time of multiculturalism's institutionalization was remarkable. For one, the administration at my college (as elsewhere) moved some money toward the diversification of the curriculum. We already had faculty onboard who could teach African history or Chinese literature, but now they were able to create minors and even majors, to secure funds for programming, and to give greater profile for the study of other places. The college also provided funds for students to create cultural organizations, to gather together to socialize for ourselves, and to conduct cultural shows for the campus. These were early days for the cultural organizations.

One of the tricks of college multiculturalism was that it gave us students of color a sense that our histories belonged to this intellectual world, indeed that we should walk with pride across the campus. But multiculturalism didn't touch the overwhelming power of "white supremacy from above," which was lodged in the bricks and mortar of our beautiful campus. I don't mean the men in white hoods, who laid terror across the country decades earlier (that's "white supremacy from below"). I mean the comfortable assumption of multiculturalism that our histories belong—but do not in any way come close to—the untouched (and generally unspoken) superiority of the cultures of Europe (and European culture in the United States). The world of multiculturalism welcomes the cultures of the other lands (Africa, Asia, Latin America) and puts them

up for display. But it is unwilling to allow this new cultural
recognition to disrupt the contented place of European culture
at the top of an unspoken hierarchy. Teach the Bhagavad Gita
and the history of Asante Kingdom, but, *come on*, it is not of
the same caliber as, say, the Bible and the history of the Renais-
sance. Include the "non-Western," but always as a subordinate,
even as we are too polite to actually make such a statement in
public.

What allows European civilization to remain untouched
by foreign hands, despite the long history of interaction and
borrowing, is the tendency to divide the world into separate
civilizations, to make the claim that these civilizations have
their own logic and that they are insulated from each other.
These unitary civilizations are all then provided with a dominant logic, with the contradictory traditions erased or at least
seen as trivial to the point of being irrelevant. These isolated
cultures, in turn, are seen to play an overwhelming role in
the lives of the individuals who are affiliated with them. For
example, Indian civilization is seen as singular, governed by
particular social rules (such as caste) that are timeless and immutable. If individuals or groups disagree with these rules, a
claim is made that they are no longer of that civilization, but
now have been, say, "Westernized." The civilization's culture
remains stable, and the actions of individuals and groups are
treated as variances from the norm. It was this static idea of
culture that grounded the concept of multiculturalism.

Much of what I've written to this point is in passive voice.
In a crafty opening to his 1984 *La Racisme*, Albert Memmi
describes racism as a "tragic enigma," in which "no one, or
almost no one, wishes to see themselves as racist; still, racism,

persists, real and tenacious." As I lay out the inner logic of multiculturalism, much the same sort of sensation occurs to me. Hidden in the core of the idea are its pernicious implications, although on the surface much of it seems bland and inoffensive. King anticipated this in a 1967 speech, when he asked his country to see integration not as a "problem but as an opportunity to participate in the beauty of diversity." This beauty is in the resources of these traditions, their wisdom as well as the struggles to reform and reconstruct social and theological life. The histories of interchange and subordination, and the contradictions within the delineated cultural worlds, are generally ignored in the mainstream rendition of multiculturalism. We are told to *respect* each other, as if condescension is a social relation we should prize. I'd prefer to struggle with cultural elements in someone else's society rather than bow down before it in the name of cultural relativism.

I guess when I say that multiculturalism has its tricks, one of them is the ability to mask the maintenance of both cultural and social hierarchy while allowing in a selection of cultural forms and its chosen people. The campus's overall hierarchical culture remains. Upward mobility is the order of the day: one has to be proud if one's own is now a corporate CEO or a military general. I suppose it was with a combination of self-righteousness and bitterness that I copied down a line from Gandhi in one of my college notebooks: "The test of orderliness in a country is not the number of millionaires it owns, but the absence of starvation among its masses" (Muir Central College Economics Society, Allahabad, December 22, 1916). I suppose also that that was why I spent more of my free time (and there was not much of that) organizing my peers against the college's investments in apartheid South Africa and volunteering at a local church basement to give a hand to the newly arrived Salvadorian political refugees. It turned out that the bulk of the Students Against Apartheid were either Indians or Mexican Americans. At our events we played the soundtrack from *Pukar* and *Coolie* and ate tacos while talking about how to get our college to disinvest (we won). These were incidental episodes, unable to overwhelm the culture of hierarchy that governed the campus. Campus politics, in its small way, might have tried to incubate a culture of solidarity, although to be fair we mostly let our marginality get in our way and ended up with self-righteousness.

What's the Matter with You, Rock?

Most Americans today are simply fed up with government at all levels.

—Richard M. Nixon, 1970

In 1972, at a White House gathering, Carl Gerstacker, head of Dow Chemical, told President Nixon, "I have long dreamed of buying an island owned by no nation and of putting the World Headquarters of Dow Company on truly neutral ground of such an island, beholden to no notion of society." That the head of a U.S.-based firm could intone such secessionist ideas in front of the U.S. president, and find approval for it, is astounding. But Nixon was receptive, even eager. He had touted the New Federalism, which included not only a genteel form of the racist "states' rights" but also, decisively, freedom for capital to operate across the country. On the first score, Nixon devolved social wage schemes to increasingly underfunded states and municipalities. Nixon's team sought to "starve the beast," where the "beast" represented the federal government, the state—the very institutions that the civil rights movement had vested its hopes in and from which it claimed its unpaid check. One administration after another would thereafter cut the funds that supported the constitutive and regulative state, invoking the mantra of "fiscal responsibility" and "balancing the budget" to undermine any effort to increase its social wage obligations. The cutbacks often took place in those areas of the state's operations that held the most promise for the widening of the aspirations of the newly enfranchised people of color, such as in the extension of housing credit, the improvement of schools, the enhancement of college scholarships, and the provision of employment opportunities in areas previously denied to people of color. "States' rights" of the Southern variety (don't mess with our right to Jim Crow) now morphed into the right of localities to undermine the federal provisions passed by the Johnson administration as a response to the civil rights movement.

The captains of industry and finance had already pledged themselves to the inevitable victory of civil rights, but the spirit of equality didn't interfere with their own concerns and projects. Most of them were liberals in that they couldn't countenance the bad behavior of racism of the Ku Klux Klan variety. That was simply gauche. But their sensibility didn't translate into a concession that the state must now redouble its efforts on other fronts to ameliorate the long night of slavery and Jim Crow. On the contrary, their sense of decency simply went so far as to prohibit any outward signs of racism, whereas their strong commitment to the private sector and individual initiative enabled them, as a class, to frown at any suggestion of an expansion of the federal disbursement. They didn't want an expansion of the social wage, certainly, but what they really wanted was elsewhere: the withdrawal of the state's "interference" in the world of money. Gerstacker's dream had already begun to be reality in Nixon's America. Regulation of corporations began to slacken, as did tax laws and other such hindrances. Through a series of complex maneuvers, the U.S. dollar gradually replaced gold as the anchor of international finance. Petro-profits and offshore funds began to be held in dollars, whose strength provided a necessary resilience to the slowly unfettered U.S. commercial banks and corporate sector. Many companies parked their legal papers in Delaware (which operates as a flagless island), in the minor islands in the Caribbean, and in various European "offshore" ports. Most of the larger firms did not need to avail themselves of such loopholes. They simply lobbied for less and less regulation: even when modest laws to protect workers and the environment and to protect shareholders and depositors remained on the books, these were summarily ignored since the state no longer possessed the capacity or will to enforce its own statutory regulations. This deregulated state is an essential part of the landscape of the post–civil rights world.

In the 1990s, I remember spending hours of my week trying to reach various federal offices, this mainly having to do with the regulation of tobacco advertisements near places where youth congregate (a real problem in oppressed neighborhoods) and with police brutality. The 202 area code seemed far from our reality. To ask for assistance from the state on matters of regulation and enforcement seemed akin to banging on a door to an empty room. The state had gone to lunch, permanently.

But not all of the state went to lunch. Powerful interests refused to allow government to increase civilian consumption and investment beyond an outer limit of around 14.6 percent of the GDP (it was 14.5 percent in 1938 and 14.6 percent in 2007). In the February 2009 issue of *Monthly Review*, the editors wrote, "The reasons for this are straightforward. Beyond some minimal level, real estate interests oppose public housing; private health care interests and medical professionals oppose public health care; insurance companies oppose public insurance programs; private education interests oppose public education; and so on. The big exceptions to this are highways and prisons within civilian government, together with military spending."

Wisely, the ruling elite opted for military and police spending and petroleum-fueled transportation networks rather than for social spending, largely because the latter would create the basis for social solidarity. If you provide universal health care and public transportation, it will link the destiny of individuals and families into a collective, which will then provide the kinds of collective feelings that threaten the basis of hierarchical power and wealth. This vast public expenditure on the military is, therefore, *rational*, and so too is the use of this military power to enforce a U.S.-based narrative of how the world should work (the iron fist is often revealed from behind the thin velvet glove). Military force has become an even more necessary component of statecraft as the United States sees its manufacturing wither and its society become addicted to credit and cheap goods from elsewhere. The United States has one main comparative advantage, its military force, which it uses as a means to maintain its authority over the planet, despite its termite-ridden financial house.

What this story traces is the development of the corporate state, riding roughshod over the social wage state. And this shift does not occur only in the United States. Indeed, this is a gradual, global process that has been given the misleading name "globalization." The term globalization refers to the breakdown of the social wage state, the release of finance capital from state constraints, the creation of a new telecommunication technology to link the planet, and the production of transportation networks (including deep-water docks) to move goods across the oceans. When you put these elements together you have a social order that is able to undermine the needs of ordinary people in the service of capital. Investment flees to areas where labor is controllable and where its costs are low, production of goods takes place only when they are needed ("just-in-time production" enables low inventories to be held by firms), and states cease to be able to properly plan for the future well-being of their societies. Globalization makes the world an island for corporate power.

Unleashed capital and unregulated businesses prey upon that wonderful resource protected for several decades by the social wage state: the commons. In the early decades of the twentieth century, social democratic states and anticolonial movements that morphed into states corralled vast sectors of social life and the landscape, designating them as the "commons" to be used by all. Education and health care, water and forests, electricity and roadways would be run by the state in the people's interests, and private profit-driven firms would be unable to control them. From the 1970s onward, these areas of social life and the landscape have been in the middle of a fight between those who want to maintain them in their public guise and those who want to privatize them. The fights are dramatic in the streets of Bolivia and in the byways of Baghdad, but they are nonetheless important in the reconstruction of New Orleans and in the giving over of vast areas of U.S. public policy to lobbyists from corporations. These are examples of how the "commons" are now the battlefield between those who believe that everything is for a profit and those who believe that at least some things are sacrosanct.

The seizure of the commons comes at a time when the entire global economy is reshaped by major technological and legal changes. Telecommunications systems and rationalized forms of transport for goods led to the possibility that firms could disarticulate the production process: no longer is a commodity necessarily made in one place, because its production can be coordinated across the oceans (cotton from Egypt is cut in Bangladesh; buttons from Brazil are put onto these shirt pieces in the Mexican maquiladoras for sale in the United States). These work sites typically hire women workers, most of whom labor without union protections or without governmental regulations. Even as these workers produce valuable goods that often require skill in the production process, their labor is degraded: they are considered to work without skill. Men who work in these jobs are also seen as de-skilled, a process of "harmonizing down"—bringing all workers to the lowest common denominator. The entire process of the degradation of work and the superexploitation of the workers is known as the "feminization of labor" (even as in some cases, such as in the agricultural sector in many countries, women have lost control of the kinds of jobs they once had to machines and to men). The U.S. service sector grows in this period along this same logic, bringing down the value given to the jobs in this sector both in terms of the pay earned by the workers and by the respect they get for their work. Add to this the use of machines to substitute for humans, whether automated technology at the service end or the robotic arms of the industrial sector. It is a miserable time to be a human being.

Globalization impacted the Atlantic world with as much ferocity as it did the rest of the planet. Factories closed their doors, and more and more workers found themselves redundant. Educational systems set up to provide the minimal literacy needed for an industrial workforce now lost their momentum: what was there to educate children toward, as jobs vanished? The hopeless at the bottom of the income scale went "off the books," into illegal occupations or into despondency. Their neighborhoods resembled prisons, with the police as the main emissary of the state and with many off to the actual prisons, whose populations burgeoned. White workers also suffered, but not at the rates of workers of color. Migrants of the upper end (H1B technical workers) and at the low end (undocumented manual laborers, and H2A and H2B temporary guest workers) faced pressure from anti-immigrant rhetoric from both those who had been the local victims of globalization (their jobs went overseas) and politicians who had engineered the simultaneous deindustrialization of North Atlantic society and the destruction of agriculture in the global south (the North American Free Trade Agreement's impact on Mexican corn is the apposite example).

A Political Recession

The mind that is not baffled is not employed.
—Wendell Berry, "The Real Work"

A son of a white mother and a black father whose middle name is Hussein and who has lived and traveled widely around the world: this is not the typical biography of a president. Even twenty years ago it would have been impossible to imagine the moment. But much has changed in the past decades. The civil rights laws of the 1960s gave full legal equality to nonwhite citizens, although this barely altered the conditions of deprivation for those who needed only glance backward to see their enslaved ancestors. Nevertheless, the new conditions of the 1980s enabled select nonwhite citizens to move into the upper reaches of the military, the academy, and the corporate world. In this postsegregated world, diversity was valued, and mainstream institutions prided themselves for hiring nonwhites. It is this change that opened the doors of Occidental College, Columbia University, and then Harvard to Barack Obama. A generation of black, Latino, and Asian youth came out of these elite institutions to positions of authority in the country's institutions. What distinguished Obama from most of those who graduated from these colleges is that he decided to relinquish the lure of Wall Street in favor of the most impoverished streets. He became a community organizer.

In *Dreams of My Father*, Obama relates how he was moved by the culture of the civil rights movement. From it he learned that "communities had to be created, fought for, tended like gardens. They expanded or contracted with the dreams of men—and in the civil rights movement those dreams had been large." His journey through the streets of Chicago to the presidency was marked by a determination to allow people to have big dreams and to tend to communities small and large. But the advantage for Obama was that his pursuit of the highest offices came at a time when diversity had become the dominant ethos. His achievement is his and his times'. He is not a black politician, someone who wins office in a predominantly black neighborhood and principally tends to the needs of the black community. He is a dark-skinned man who leads a nation that has come to terms with the fact of diversity.

Obama's victory is not, however, a victory over racism or social turmoil. The police will continue to discriminate against black drivers; bank officials will continue to snub black buyers in what are seen as white neighborhoods. The petty insults and the meaningful discriminations have not been overcome by his ascent. Indeed, it has even spawned resentment. What we have is what King called "the stagnant equality of sameness"; integration with resentment is not a community. It is stagnant because there is little hope of transcending the resentment; it is sameness because there is no understanding that historical inequalities cannot be simply wished away. Indeed, these inequalities have hardened. Obama has not moved an agenda to change the social landscape. He is a president of the racist status quo.

OBAMABAD

In 2007, the Illinois government renamed a major freeway that links the wealthy suburbs of northern Chicago the Jane Addams Memorial Tollway. This roadway runs though the heart of northern Chicago's urban sprawl, the expanse of concrete and glass that makes up corporate headquarters (Motorola and United Airlines) and megashopping centers (the Woodfield Mall and the Huntley Prime Outlets). Addams, a famous social reformer, would probably not have taken kindly to her name being tied to these churches of American capitalism. The town of Schaumburg sits in the middle of this "Golden Corridor," and in the middle of this town is the India House Restaurant.

On October 31, 2008, a Konkani businessman, Raghuveer Nayak, booked the India House for a private party. He hosted luminaries of Chicago's business community, people such as pharmacy owners Harish and Renuka Bhatt, hotelier Satish "Sonny" Gabhawala, as well as prominent political leaders of the Indian American community, such as Babu Patel and Iftekhar Shareef (both past presidents of the Federation of Indian Associations). Nayak, also a former head of the Federation of Indian Associations, owns a group of surgical centers. A highly regarded Democratic Party fund-raiser, Nayak is also a friend of another person who attended the lunch, Rajinder Bedi, an aide to then–Illinois governor Rod Blagojevich (Blagojevich called Bedi "My Sikh Warrior"). In addition, among the few who were not Indian American, the party included Congressman Jesse Jackson Jr.'s brother, Jonathan. Governor Blagojevich made a brief appearance.

People who attended the party made it clear that Nayak

brought them together to put his friend Congressman Jesse Jackson Jr.'s name up for the Senate. It had become clear that Barack Obama would win the presidential contest to be held the next week, and these deep pockets realized that his elevation would open the Senate seat. The governor of Illinois would have the right to fill the seat until the next election cycle. Nayak, Bedi, Bhatt, and others wanted to put in a good word for their friend, Congressman Jackson. Gabhawala told the *Chicago Tribune* that he saw Bedi and Nayak try to convince Babu Patel, a Blagojevich fund-raiser, to use his influence and money on Jackson's behalf. In a country whose highest court decided that political donations are a form of free speech, it is to be expected that you can't put in a word for someone without opening your wallet. No wonder that in December 1971 the editors of *Newsweek* wryly said, "The relationship between money and politics is so organic that seeking reform is tantamount to asking a doctor to perform open-heart surgery on himself." According to a federal indictment and to sources at the meeting, the fund-raisers promised to raise over a million dollars for Blagojevich, who would then nominate Jackson to fill Obama's Senate seat. Later that day, a federal government wiretap caught the governor saying, "We were approached pay-to-play, that, you know, he'd raise me five hundred grand. An emissary came. Then the other guy would raise a million, if I made him a senator."

On December 4, the governor met with "Advisor B" (as he is named in the criminal complaint), and told him that "Senate Candidate 5" (Jesse Jackson Jr.) would get "greater consideration" because of a surety that no. 5 would help Blagojevich raise money, and that he would give Blagojevich "some [money] up front, maybe." Blagojevich wanted something "tangible" now, because "some of this stuff's gotta start happening now . . . right now . . . and we gotta see it. You understand?" Two days later, a month after Obama's election, the principal fund-raisers from the India House gathering came to a suburban home in Elmhurst, another of the wealthy suburban towns that ring Chicago. Here, according to the *Chicago Tribune*, the Indian American businessmen discussed raising $1 million to $1.5 million. At the October 31 fund-raiser, Nayak had already made it clear to Bhatt that he could find half a million, but Bhatt and others would have to come up with the other half million. The December 4 meeting apparently made this vision reality.

Right after Obama's election, Blagojevich said, "I want to make some money." He was agnostic about whom he would nominate to Obama's seat as long as he would get some tangible benefit from the act. Obama's team, by all accounts, refused to barter the seat, although questions remain about the contact between Obama's chief of staff Rahm Emanuel and the Blagojevich people. Jackson says that he had limited contact with Blagojevich, and when the scandal broke, he said, "I did not initiate nor authorize anyone, at any time, to promise anything to Gov. Blagojevich on my behalf. I never sent a message or an emissary to the governor to make an offer or to propose a deal about the U.S. Senate seat." Federal officials arrested Blagojevich on December 9 on charges of corruption. He was found guilty and, as of this writing, waits to be sentenced to prison.

What, No Envelope?

The spotlight turned, briefly, on the Indian American community in Chicago. These men, Nayak, Bhatt, and Bedi, were a sideshow to the greater scandals, which were how much Jackson knew and what kind of contact Obama's transition team had with Blagojevich. Over the years Blagojevich and Jackson cultivated the increasingly affluent Indian American community in Chicago. Blagojevich had a fruitful relationship with the banker Amrish Mahajan and his wife, the businesswoman Anita Mahajan. "Uncle Amrish," as many know him, came to his prominence through his close ties with the Parrillo family (a political clan that is linked to the Chicago mafia). Mahajan rose to the head of the Mutual Bank, whose well-heeled customers donated money to politicians anointed by the Mahajans. Blagojevich was a major beneficiary, as money entered his campaign war chest and his wife, Patti, earned huge real estate contracts from the Mahajan circle. In 2007, the government arrested and charged Anita Mahajan with overbilling the state for millions of dollars on her state contract. Harish Bhatt, who called himself the "Joe Nobody from Joliet," has had his pharmacies under investigation for four years. The government seeks evidence that Bhatt's fund-raising for Blagojevich turned into phone calls to regulators to back off from their investigation of fraud (the main source, Jim Thorns, died of cancer in 2006, and the main regulator, Yashwant Amin, got his job through Bhatt's say-so; the entire story tells us a bit about the sordidness of business and politics in our current time).

All of this frazzled the Indian American community. Nayak is a well-regarded businessman and a philanthropist. His charity includes setting up hospitals in India and raising funds for tsunami relief. Nayak's closest ties are with the Jackson family. He won the Push Excellence in Public Service award from Jesse Jackson's Operation PUSH, and accompanied Jackson to India in November 2007 (Nayak organized a lecture by Jackson at New Delhi's Jawaharlal Nehru University). In addition, Nayak brought the main Chicago Democrats into the India Caucus, and was a booster for the Indo-U.S. nuclear deal. Nayak, Mahajan, Bedi, Bhatt, and others are all close allies who have leveraged their political connections for economic gain and used that money to strengthen their political heft.

Everything that the Indian Americans did is customary. Political campaigns have become overwhelmingly expensive. The 2008 presidential race cost more than $1 billion. In addition, elected officials live within the social confines of the very wealthy, and often aspire to their lifestyle. Even as more and more millionaires run for public office, the bulk of the elected officials do not come from family wealth. Their jobs do not provide them with the six- or seven-figure salaries that they'd need to fulfill their upwardly mobile aspirations. Scandals are now commonplace. The fallout from the sleazy pay-to-play empire set up by the lobbyist Jack Abramoff continues to resonate through Washington, D.C., notably inside the Republican Party (many of whose elected officials, such as Congressman Randy Cunningham, are now in prison).

Near my town, in western Massachusetts, a contractor goes to see the local mayor to deliver his regular payment of $5,000. The mayor, Richard Goyette, stops him. "What, no envelope?" he asks, stuffing the money into his pockets. In a federal wiretap, Goyette complains about those who had to pay him to

earn city contracts: "They're all greedy." The symbiotic relationship between money and power is evident regardless of
the scale—from a small municipal contract to the large no-bid
contracts for firms to operate in Iraq (such as Vice President
Cheney's Halliburton).

The sleaze is characteristic of American politics, and it is
one of the principal reasons for the lack of faith among the population for their elected officials and for the political process in
general. Large numbers of people refuse to vote on election
day for precisely the reason that they do not trust the process.
Their withdrawal allows the connected and the wealthy to cyn-
ically make the system their own. The Supreme Court decided
in 2010 that corporations are persons; their right and enthusiasm to vote seems to carry more water than do the aspirations of the many. Obama's election in 2008 raised hopes, and
brought large numbers of people to the polls. Millions hoped
that it would turn the page on the corruption at all levels of
government. The Blagojevich scandal and the *Citizens United*
lawsuit on corporate personhood are a few of the many reality
checks, a reminder of how widespread corruption has become.

Blagojevich's various scandals are quite pedestrian in today's
America. In one, he wanted a payoff for the expansion of the
Jane Addams Tollway. That deal didn't happen over samosas
and masala tea. But others did. When Obama won, Blagojevich recognized quickly that he had a "golden" opportunity, a
goose that could lay a million eggs in one swoop. The larger
the deal, the less the squalor. Three of the past six Illinois gov-
ernors spent time in jail for corruption, so the odds were always
against Blagojevich. His affinity with the Indian Americans is
not just for their money, but also because both share the hunger

of immigrants (Blagojevich is the son of a Serbian immigrant and a working-class American woman). Just as Bedi, Nayak, Bhatt, and Mahajan turned to Blagojevich for their ascent, he was gifted by marriage to the politically connected Mell family. Money, power, family: this is as much a Hollywood drama as it is a Bollywood drama.

THE REPUBLICANS' OBAMA

In 1996, I got into a debate in the pages of *India West* with Asha Knott of Southern California's Republican Party about the candidacy of Nimi McConigley for the U.S. Senate. The Republicans ran advertisements in the community papers appealing to desis to send "one of us" to the "most powerful body in the country" and to "create history by putting the first India-born person in the U.S. Senate."

Nimi McConigley, a Wyoming state representative, was a founding patron of the Asian American Republican Club and had this to say of her long tenure in the Republican Party: "Twenty years ago, I was proud to be an American because I believed in the values and principles on which this nation was founded. The Republican Party offers the hope to make America the nation that so many of us from other countries saw as the land of freedom, opportunity, and hope." This comment was made in 1995, when Newt Gingrich's House of Representatives tried its best to squelch all opportunity for immigrants and pushed the Clinton administration to pass the draconian 1996 immigration act. McConigley's most egregious position was her support for English-only legislation — cold comfort to most immigrants: even those of us who speak English (with a foreign accent) benefit from the liberal climate created toward all immigrants by policies such as bilingual education. The English-only movement was a thinly veiled attack on all immigrants. How many non–English speakers live in Wyoming anyway? McConigley also displayed impatience toward the poor, calling them "people who use lack of money as an excuse for their inability to get the job done." When McConigley said that her hero was Gandhi, one could only wonder what the great man would have thought about her heartlessness toward those who are not only less fortunate but whose hard work make this world possible.

Fortunately, she lost the election.

The compulsion to support someone because of ethnicity is false.

Nevertheless, you'd have to be made of stone not to feel something at the inauguration of Bobby Jindal as Louisiana's governor on January 14, 2008. Jindal is the first nonwhite leader of Louisiana since Reconstruction. The only other nonwhite person to rule from Baton Rouge was Pinckney Stewart Pinchback, 1872–73, the first African American to serve as governor of any state in the nation, although he was not elected but promoted on the death of his predecessor.

Jindal, whose family comes from Punjab, is the first Indian American governor. Indian American groups across the country greeted his victory. The Indian American Leadership Initiative put out the most amusing statement: "Bobby Jindal replaces the Mardi Gras Indians as the best known Indian from Louisiana." A spokesperson for the National Federation of Indian American Associations said, "It is a great moment in the history of America when someone who looks like us becomes the governor of Louisiana. We should all be dancing in the street to display our pride." Jindal's victory had little to do with his being Indian American, however. A longtime conservative Republican, this young man ascended rapidly from Bush appointee to U.S. congressman to governor in little more than a decade. President Bush hastened to congratulate Jindal for his "incredible honor."

Piyush Jindal was born in Baton Rouge in 1971 to graduate-student parents. Attracted by the television show *The Brady Bunch*, four-year-old Piyush took the name of one of its characters, Bobby. As a teenager he converted to Roman Catholicism (his parents remain Hindus). All this indicates his remarkable drive. This self-direction was soon profitably yoked to an insatiable ambition. A Rhodes Scholarship at Oxford University followed college at the prestigious Brown University. Armed with the best academic credentials, Bobby joined the global consulting firm McKinsey & Company. At Oxford, Bobby studied political science, and it was politics that drew him away from the world of money. In 1995, at twenty-four, Bobby Jindal was appointed to head Louisiana's Department of Health and Human Services. Within two years, Jindal's stewardship of the agency erased its considerable budget, at enormous human cost. Louisiana dropped from forty-eighth to fiftieth (last) in the national health care rankings during Jindal's tenure. Louisiana's own health care agency reports that part of the problem was the slashing of funding for a robust set of state hospitals and outpatient primary care facilities. These are the very sections that Jindal sliced in order to bring his agency into fiscal health.

Jindal's fiscal success attracted admirers in the Bush White

House, where he was brought to head the National Bipartisan Commission on the Future of Medicare, the government health insurance system. The commission provided no final recommendations for the system's reform, although it suggested that the government raise the eligibility age for access to the system (which would mean that one would have to be older yet before being able to benefit from the insurance scheme). As the commission stalled, Jindal returned to Louisiana to run the state university system. Before he could settle in, the Bush White House called him back to Washington to be the assistant secretary of the Department of Health and Human Services. Once more, before he could get going he returned to Louisiana to run for governor against the popular Democrat Kathleen Babineaux Blanco in 2003. The Republican establishment endorsed Jindal, as Bush's proxy, but he could not defeat Blanco. Jindal nevertheless won a safe Republican seat to the U.S. Congress the following year. As soon as he won this seat, he quietly began his campaign against Blanco, which meant that he spent a lot of time in Louisiana and tried to make as few waves in Congress as possible. (He did, however, cast some crucial votes against bills on medical insurance that would have crossed pharmaceutical companies, his major financial backer.) As you can see, Jindal's career was built for him. He had no time to accomplish anything significant in any of his posts. What is significant is his rapid rise.

Hurricane Katrina struck the Gulf Coast in 2005, and the aftermath's very poorly planned recovery dented Blanco's popularity. Jindal remained silent in this period, speaking banalities rather than making any direct assault on the shabby reconstruction effort for the population (which would have also indicted his patron, President Bush). Blanco's tarnished star forced her to withdraw from the gubernatorial race in 2007, leaving the field open to Jindal.

One reason Jindal did not defeat Blanco in 2003 was that he was unable to draw the full weight of the white vote. Many conservative whites preferred to vote for a white Cajun ("native" Louisianan) Democrat than an Indian American (born in Louisiana) conservative Republican. It should be borne in mind that the leader of the Ku Klux Klan, David Duke, won 44 percent of the Republican vote in a 1990 primary election (60 percent of the white vote); a year later, Duke repeated this feat, and bragged, "I won my constituency. I won 55 percent of the white vote." Despite having the second largest African American population in the United States (after neighboring Mississippi), Louisiana's politics are structured around the ability of a statewide candidate to draw the white vote.

Racist vigilante violence marks the state's history. After the Civil War ended in 1865, for example, some local legislators considered a change in the state's constitution that might allow blacks the franchise. Recalcitrant citizens formed the White League, whose violent tactics succeeded in ending any talk of equality. It was in New Orleans that Homer Plessy, a light-skinned black man, was removed from a train in 1892 because he sat in a "whites only" section. The *Plessy v. Ferguson* case went to the U.S. Supreme Court, which decided that blacks and whites should have separate facilities although these should be equal (the "separate but equal" statute). In New Orleans, as well, a black man, Oliver Bush, began a court case to get his son, Earl, into an all-white school. Eventually, in 1954, the U.S. Supreme Court decided in *Brown v. Board*

of Education that Jim Crow segregation of this kind is illegal
and should be abolished. Drawing energy from this decision,
a young Martin Luther King Jr. and his fellow liberal clergy
formed the Southern Christian Leadership Conference in
New Orleans in 1957. In response, the White Citizens' Council, an organization of the landed white aristocracy of the region, announced, "Integration is the Southern expression of
Communism." King and others took the fight against racism to
the doorstep of the enemy.

When Hurricane Katrina struck, it revealed the rot of a racist, segregated society. King's movement ended de jure segregation, but it did little against de facto segregation and inequality.
Almost 20 percent of Louisiana's residents live beneath the
U.S. poverty line, and a dramatic number of blacks live not
only in poverty but also in jail. The incarceration rate in New
Orleans, where most blacks in the state live, is twice that of the
U.S. rate: 1,480 prisoners per 100,000 residents. Katrina tore
through the city and state, exposing the inequality and shock-
ing the nation. Blacks make up close to 84 percent of the city's
population, but if you went only to the French Quarter or to
the upmarket and highland residential districts, you'd miss this
fact. Since the days of slavery, blacks have lived in the *battures*,
the back-swamp areas where they have enjoyed neither flood
protection nor property ownership. Most of the black population lived in substandard federal housing, and since the 1990s,
the government has sought to evict them from these as well. In
New Orleans in the late 1990s, the city went after St. Thomas
Project, which abutted an affluent white neighborhood. The
war against the black poor had rarely seemed so blatant. The
fate of blacks in New Orleans should remind us of other

"disposable people" (about 1.5 billion across the planet) who live in slums, work in alternative economies, and earn the disdain and fear of the well heeled. The distance between these people and the aristocrats who run the system became clear when the then-president's mother, Barbara Bush, faced the nation after her visit with refugees in Houston, Texas. "What I'm hearing, which is sort of scary, is they all want to stay in Texas. Everyone is so overwhelmed by the hospitality. And so many of the people in the [Houston Arena] here, you know, were underprivileged anyway, so this is working very well for them." They should, in other words, be pleased that the hurricane allowed them to live in better conditions than before.

Bobby Jindal, then a congressman, held his tongue. His main carp was not against the Bush administration that had sent the bulk of the state's National Guard to Iraq (leaving their posts absent when the disaster struck), nor was it against the long history of inequality revealed by the aftermath. Jindal decided to speak out against the "red tape" of the government response. Katrina, which had come to mean the racism of the federal and state government, provided the young congressman with an opportunity to champion less government and more "faith-based" reconstruction solutions. No word about the dispossession of his fellow citizens, and little care that the white elites were now moving to grab the land which once housed a large black population. Scott Crow, who worked in the reconstruction of the city, recalls how white militias roamed the city after Katrina, making sure to run blacks out of town: "These white militias made it their jobs to secure law and order in the absence of the police. Their brand of justice was to intimidate any black person walking on the street alone, or in any number that was smaller than the militia." Blanco's inaction compromised her; Jindal's silence on issues of racism enamored him to a section of the white voters.

As the election campaign heated up, a terrible incident in the town of Jena, Louisiana, brought national attention to the enduring racism in the state. When white students intimidated black students at Jena High School (by hanging nooses on a tree and by pointing shotguns at them), the school authorities blamed the black students for making trouble. The police joined the administration and in the course of an altercation arrested and jailed six black students. The case of the Jena Six (all teenagers) angered the nation. On September 20, 2007, thousands of people converged on the town to demand their release. Bobby Jindal, in the thick of his election battle, took a strong stand against the demonstrations. "We certainly don't need any outside agitators coming in here," he said. The phrase "outside agitator" has a long lineage in the anti–civil rights movement and within the White Citizens' Councils. Jindal's heavy-handed code sent a strong message to the racist vote that he could be trusted not to "pander" to the black population. Jena is in LaSalle Parish, whose white voters overwhelmingly voted for David Duke in 1991. This time Jindal carried that vote, winning the parish with a handy 55 percent (his closest opponent, Walter Boasso won short of 15 percent). "Don't let anyone talk bad about Louisiana," Jindal said as he claimed his victory. In other words, don't talk about racism. "Those days are officially over."

A few days after the victory, Reverend Nehemiah Thompson of the National Association of Asian Indian Christians wrote a letter to the *New York Times*. Rev. Thompson's advice was simple: "Go easy on conservatism. Ideology is a luxury of the upper class. But rebuild New Orleans. Care about the poor, the children, the elderly, the unemployed, blacks, and Hispanics." Jindal's program, however, opposes stem cell research and abortion and is in favor of "faith-based" public policy and corporate solutions to social problems (his election coffers were lined by oil magnate donations). The test for Jindal was during the BP Gulf oil spill in 2010, when he fell flat on his knees. A presidential panel report, released in January 2011, had some startling news, arguing that Jindal seemed more interested in his media image than in relief and reconstruction: "Coast Guard responders watched Governor Jindal—and the TV cameras following him—return to what appeared to be the same spot of oiled marsh day after day to complain about the inadequacy of the federal response, even though only a small amount of marsh was then oiled," the report noted. "When the Coast Guard sought to clean up that piece of affected marsh, Governor Jindal refused to confirm its location," a Coast Guard official told the investigators. Jindal's office said this was a "ridiculous" assertion, but it did not have more specifics to dispel the charge.

Other Indian Americans shared Rev. Thompson's concerns. Deepa Iyer, the head of South Asian American Leaders of Tomorrow, said just after his election, "Bobby Jindal should not get a free pass solely because he is of Indian descent." She was concerned about his civil rights record. During his time in Congress, Jindal voted against hate crimes legislation and for strict immigration enforcement. As the governor of Louisiana, Iyer said, "Jindal will have to confront some of these issues." But will his confrontation be in the vein of Bush or, as

Rev. Thompson put it, will Jindal "teach and practice what Jesus taught: nonviolence, compassion for the poor and the oppressed, and healing of sick [health care for all]"? Iyer, who sat next to Jindal at an *India Abroad* event, would be the first to attest that he does not have the temperament of Bush. Bush had a blatant disregard for human society, and for humanity. When Bush was governor of Texas he presided over 152 executions and mocked one of his victims, Karla Faye Tucker. In 1999, after Tucker's execution, journalist Tucker Carlson asked Bush whether he had talked to her, and Bush said that there was no point. What would she say, he asked. " 'Please,' Bush whimpers, his lips pursed in mock desperation, 'don't kill me.' " Carlson was horrified by Bush's "flashes of meanness." None of this is in Jindal. What we have instead is a callous disregard for the social costs of far-Right positions.

In 2003, Congressman Joe Wilson of the India Caucus wrote in *India Abroad* that Bobby Jindal "is the Indian American community's future." Nikki Haley, who is now governor of South Carolina and whose family also migrated from Punjab, once said, "Does it matter for the Indian community whether a candidate is Republican or Democrat? What we need is more people in political office. The candidate's party affiliation is irrelevant for us as a community, at this time." But that is the heart of the matter: Are people like Jindal the future of a community? And don't their political views matter? Or does one support them by the compulsions of ethnicity? At what point do we recoil from a political bloc, the right wing, whose candidates, such as Republican Karen Balderston, say of their opponents (in her case, the highly regarded Swati Dandekar of

Iowa), "While I was growing up in Iowa, learning and reciting the pledge of allegiance to the flag, Swati was growing up in India under the still-existent caste system. How can that prepare her for legislating in Iowa or any other part of our great United States?"

What is clear is that, as with Obama, Jindal's personhood is more compelling than his actual political program. Young and charismatic, with a promise to be postracial and yet with dark skin: that is the temptation of both Jindal and Obama. Their politics are not part of the equation, only what they represent symbolically. As men of color, both need to be taken seriously for who they are, not simply for what they look like. If we take Jindal seriously, we find him to be not so far removed from Balderston or Sarah Palin—those whose agendas are against the right of a woman to control her body, against science, against secularism, for guns, for war.

Two years after Jindal graduated from Brown University, on the morning of September 30, 1993, a terrible earthquake (magnitude 6.3) struck the Latur and Osmanabad districts of Maharashtra. The Indian government later said that close to eight thousand people had died and that over thirty thousand homes had been destroyed. The scale of the earthquake was very significant.

A few hours after the earthquake had struck, I got a phone call from a student at Brown University, Pooja Sarin. Several months before the call, Pooja and Raj Dave of the South Asian Students Association (SASA) from Brown had contacted me. They were the ones who came to my office at Direct Action for Rights and Equality, asking for a way to be useful. This time Pooja wanted to do something, anything, to help those who had survived the earthquake and whose lives needed to be rebuilt.

In the typically organized fashion of college students, SASA gathered for a daily fund drive in the Brown post office and collected money, and held a fund-raising dinner one evening not long after the earthquake. The money was sent to a relief agency in India, and it turns out that some homes had been built for their effort. When I remember these Brown students, I think of them as the Latur Generation: they had already held numerous political workshops on campus and many of them had been involved in the effort to make Brown more democratic (to allow community people to use the library, for instance, and to ensure that it admitted students independent of their means to pay). When they hosted the eighth annual SASA Conference in March 1996, they made sure to include political discussions that are often not heard at the mainly social, partying SASA.

I remember many of these students with joy. Jindal spent his time with the Christian Fellowship, not with SASA. There was no need for him to have been at the SASA events. He had the right to make his choices. There is no compulsion to inhabit your ethnicity in an organized fashion, as there should be no compulsion to support political figures because of their inherited ancestry. But Jindal nonetheless had the moxie of the Latur Generation. He was a smart aleck who, when once asked by his elementary school teacher, "Why is it that all Indians are so smart and well-behaved?" answered, "It was the food."

OBAMA'S INDIAN

Barack Obama's victory in the U.S. presidential election warmed the hearts of millions around the world. When Jesse Jackson wept in Grant Park on the night that Obama declared victory, many cried with him. I had worked for Jackson's campaign in 1988. With Jackson's defeat came the long hibernation of American progressivism in the electoral domain (but for brief bursts of misplaced enthusiasm for Bill Clinton, and then, for a section of the Left, hard work to move a third-party agenda, largely behind Ralph Nader's runs for president). Obama's run for president took hold of that tradition. A few days after his victory, Obama announced his transition team. The names were not from the progressive tradition but from the more cautious, even conservative side of the Democratic Party. To lead the effort Obama chose a Washington insider, John Podesta, who had since 2003 set up a government-in-exile at the Center for American Progress (CAP). Many CAP fellows were veterans of the Clinton years or long-term staffers on the Hill for the Democratic warhorses. There were others, fresh-faced in Washington with glowing references from the Ivy League. Their hibernation ended with Obama's election. They waited for their assignments in the new administration.

In the list of the transition team, I spotted the name Sonal Shah. I wrote an essay for *Counterpunch* calling attention to Sonal Shah's affiliations with various Hindutva groups. In this viral age, essays such as this leave their locale and take on a life of their own. This one created a little kerfuffle. People excited by the prospect of the Obama victory and by the ascension of an Asian American—a South Asian American no less—to a position of authority were miffed that I had rained on their parade. Some claimed that I had stooped to the Sarah Palin tactic of guilt by association. Just because Shah's parents are closely affiliated with the Hindutva groups does not mean that she is associated with them, they said. I agree. Matters got more serious when former Republican senator Rick Santorum (Latin for plagiarist) took my article and recycled it in the *Philadelphia Inquirer.* Under pressure, Sonal Shah released a statement against "baseless and silly reports" on the Internet. She forthrightly pointed out that her "personal politics have nothing in common with the views espoused by the Vishwa Hindu Parishad (VHP), the Rashtriya Swayamsevak Sangh (RSS), or any such organization." Shah's statement seemed to settle the issue. It was gratifying to those who wanted this fracas to die and for her to move into the limelight of the Obama administration (there was even a rumor that she might be offered a cabinet post).

In Washington, Shah has another reputation. There she is known for her Democratic credentials, most of which seem to lie somewhere between neoliberalism and welfare liberalism. The bleeding heart pauses but then ticks again to the tune of pragmatism. Shah, a product of the University of Chicago (as I am), shined her corporate shoes at Anderson Consulting (which I did not do), and then went into Clinton's Treasury Department, where she helped Treasury Secretary Robert Rubin put a U.S. stamp on the post-1997 Asian economic recovery. The corporate side was balanced with an interest in the ideology of "giving back." When Bush took office in 2001, Shah went to the Center for Global Development and while there joined her brother, Anand, in forming Indicorps. Knowing full well the desire among many South Asian Americans to give back to their homeland, the Shahs created an organization to help them go and volunteer in India, to do for them what the Peace Corps did for young liberals in the 1960s and 1970s. Shah went to Goldman Sachs and then to Google. Shah is not different from many CAP liberals, who honed their dexterity trying to reconcile the irreconcilable: capital and freedom, private accumulation and human needs.

But there is a less typical side to Shah's story. Born in Gujarat, Shah came to the United States as a two-year-old. Her father, a chemical engineer, first worked in New York before moving to Houston and then moving away from his education toward the stock market. The Shahs remain active in Houston's Indian community, not only in the ecumenical Gujarati Samaj (a society for people from Gujarat), but also in the far more cruel organizations of the Hindu Right, such as the VHP of America (VHPA), the Overseas Friends of the BJP (the main political party of the Hindu Right), and Ekal Vidyalaya. Shah's parents, Ramesh and Kokila, not only work as volunteers for these outfits, they also held positions of authority in them. Their daughter was not far behind. She too was an active member of the VHPA, the U.S. branch of the most virulently fascistic outfit within India. The VHP's head, Ashok Singhal, believes that his organization should "inculcate a fear psychosis among [India's] Muslim community." This was Shah's boss. Until 2001, Shah was the national coordinator of the VHPA.

Sonal Shah's statement claimed that she was not a part of the VHPA, and that her "personal politics" did not share the values of these groups. D.C.'s cohesive bloc of desi activists hastened to her defense, and many wrote me private e-mails saying that I was going after the wrong person. (One wrote, "There is so much wrong in the world, even if Sonal was a fraction of the threat you suggest, there are others far worse and better positioned than her to contend with. Stop chasing windmills, my friend—Sonal Shah is one of the good guys".) But the facts belied her disavowal.

While at the Clinton Treasury Department, Sonal Shah was on the governing council of the VHPA. In an e-mail conversation on the VHPA's Listserv in May 1998, Shah proposed that the VHPA follow the example of the Indian branch of the VHP: "Why don't we focus on improving the lives of its citizens, etc. That's where VHP Bharat's strength is—people remember that." Another e-mail refers to a "long talk" between Shah and VHPA's leader, Vijay Pallod, who calls Shah part of the VHPA's "new generation." Shah has refused to respond to questions about this e-mail.

Shah said that she left the VHPA in 2001, after she helped it with the earthquake relief for the Kutch, Gujarat, earthquake. The VHP's Shyam Tiwari said, "Sonal was a member of the VHP of America at the time of the earthquake. Her membership has expired." But three years later, Shah continued to work closely with the VHPA and its assorted mass outfits. In 2004, she delivered the keynote address to the Hindu Swayamsevak Sangh's youth conference. The HSS is the U.S. branch of the RSS, which scholar Martha Nussbaum calls "possibly the most successful fascist movement in any contemporary democracy." In November 2004, the hard Right government in Gujarat honored Shah with the Pride of Gujarat (Gujarat Garima) award. Sonal Shah could not attend, but her brother was there to get the award from Prime Minister Atal Bihari Vajpayee in the presence of Gujarat's chief minister, the RSS leader Narendra Modi. Of course others have received this award, including leading captains of industry. But they make no pretense of morality and progressivism. They are plainly opportunistic, eager for better business deals in Gujarat. The Shahs and Indicorps are different. Their agenda is putatively moral. At none of these events did the Shahs raise their voices for the broken heart and bodies of their native state. By 2004, even mainstream human rights organizations and media outlets had recognized that the Gujarat riots were state engineered, and that their author was Narendra Modi. In 2005, the U.S. government refused to allow Mr. Modi a visa on these grounds.

In 2004, I ran into Shah at the South Asian Awareness Network conference in Ann Arbor, Michigan. At a panel, I questioned her links to the Hindu Right, and so asked people to be wary about her organization, Indicorps. She was furious, and we had a bitter exchange in the green room. But at no point did she deny her active connections to the Hindu Right. Her brother, Anand, wrote to me not long after, concerned that Indicorps, which he runs full time from India, would be tainted by our tussle. "I was curious about Sonal's own personal relationship with the VHPA," I wrote back. "That sparked some concern for me. Of course we are free to have our multiple associations, and there is no expectation that all our affiliations necessarily influence each other. That necessity is granted, although it is my understanding that the VHPA is a very disciplined organization that demands a lot from its members— notably congruence in all the work that they do. Which is why I raised the question."

Gujarat was once a tolerant society, made vibrant by its role in the Indian Ocean trade. People of all faiths lived there with the kind of premodern conviviality that did not always include respect for each other but which did not at least dissolve into the kind of virulence on display in recent years. Certainly, oppressed castes bore the full brunt of an unequal social order, but even for them there was escape into Islam or into small sects of Hinduism and its offshoots, and there was a history of protest against the madness of caste rigidity. Gujarat gave us Gandhi, who went off to South Africa to learn his politics and returned to his state in 1915 to incubate the massive nationwide movement he was to lead. In November 1917, Gandhi launched a major campaign among the Gujarati peasantry at the town of Godhra. He began his meeting there by tearing up the oath of loyalty to the king, making it clear that the new grammar of Indian politics did not require such obeisance. From Godhra, charged Gandhian activists went into other villages to organize the peasantry against the many abuses of colonialism. The uprising that resulted, historian David Hardiman points out, made the area "the strongest center of rural nationalism in India." From Godhra, in 1917, went the quiet fury of freedom.

In 2002, other elements came out of Godhra, showing us how today's Gujarat differs from its own history. This time Godhra was the flashpoint not for rural protest against tyranny but for the forces of Hindu fascism. A disputed train fire that killed fifty-eight people (most of whom were activists of the Hindu Right) led to a massive pogrom against impoverished Muslim families and modestly well-off Muslim merchants. Even the normally reticent Human Rights Watch could not hold back, and its report's title revealed not only the anger of the investigators but also their own principal finding: "*We Have*

No Orders to Save You": State Participation and Complicity in Communal Violence in Gujarat (April 2002). The Hindu Right let loose its warriors, who killed two thousand people and displaced several thousand more. The state apparatus either stood by or actively participated in the torment. Investigators who traced the line of violence routinely met people who told them, "They killed my whole family." The carnage was ghastly. Historian Tanika Sarkar wrote of a "breathless climate of terror," as people fled their homes for poorly managed relief camps, afraid not only of the organized mob but also of the police. People couldn't sleep, afraid that their tormentors would come again. Chief Minister Narendra Modi came to one area and told the terrified residents, "You will be taken care of." The language chills: he might have meant that the state will protect them, or that it would punish them. His scowl and his brazen defense of his mobs was no comfort.

Gujarat remains a manufacturing center, but in the 1970s the social basis of industry changed. From the 1910s to the 1970s, the textile factories hired large numbers of workers, most of whom were members of the Gandhian trade union, the Majoor Mahajan Sangh (MMS). They had their various grouses with the system, but most had grown accustomed to the rhythms of industrial society. When a major riot between Hindus and Muslims broke out in the Gujarati city of Ahmedabad in 1969, the police moved their headquarters to the MSS office, and the union and the state jointly helped to calm things down. But in the 1970s, the large textile factories snuffed their fires, sending their workers from the formal into the informal economy. The social infrastructure of the towns and cities collapsed. Workers went into the piecework economy, driving the economic fortunes of the big businessmen through the roof but at the cost of the workers' health and social dignity. Globalization had arrived in Gujarat.

Disgruntled workers left the MSS and regrouped in the newly aggressive Hindu Right, which welcomed their grievances and reshaped their dignity around hatred of Muslims and oppressed castes. The riots of the 1990s were a dress rehearsal for the pogrom of 2002. Lumpen-capitalism led to the social collapse of Gujarat. In mid-March 2002, a few weeks after the pogrom, sociologist Jan Breman went to meet the MSS secretary general, who sorrowfully recounted his inability to reach the police during the killings. It is a sign of the eclipse of the Gandhian platform in favor of what has been called the Vedic Taliban.

The Vedic Taliban includes not only the BJP, the party in power during the Gujarat killings, but also a host of organizations known as the Sangh Parivar. These include groups whose U.S. affiliates drew in Sonal Shah's parents, and to which she also gave her time and energy. This is not in the distant past. In 2004, while at CAP, Sonal Shah gave the keynote address in Miami for the Ekal Vidyalaya Foundation of USA. Ekal Vidyalaya is an organization given over to "education" in tribal areas of India. It is the policy of Ekal Vidyalaya to organize tribal peoples into the "Hindu community" and to eschew the Christianity and animism that many practice. Ekal Vidyalaya starts schools in tribal areas and offer their students a generous dose of RSS ideology. Mohan Lal, an Ekal Vidyalaya teacher, told journalist T.K. Rajalakshmi, "We go for the RSS shakha [branch] meetings regularly. The teachers are selected only if they subscribe to the RSS way of thought." The climate created by Ekal Vidyalaya and the VHP in the tribal areas of India led to the massacres of Indian Christians (most spectacularly during Christmas 1998, as documented by Human Rights Watch in its 1999 report, *Politics by Other Means: Attacks Against Christians in India*). Sonal Shah's father Ramesh was in charge of Ekal Vidyalaya in the United States. She didn't take the time in Miami to raise these concerns. Rather, she talked about her Indicorps project, which has sent volunteers to work with groups like Ekal Vidyalaya (at least in its first year). The language of social justice and cultural rights works well to cover over the fascism that is otherwise being promoted.

No wonder that when Shah was chosen by Obama to join his team, *Rajasthan Patrika*, a newspaper from a small town (Kota) in Rajasthan, ran a statement by the local RSS and VHP leaders:

No matter what—let the Indian Congress government appease minorities [Muslims]. President Obama has shown determination by appointing a proud member of the VHP, the daughter of Ramesh Shah, a very senior VHP leader, in his team. After all, American NRIs have really helped the Hindu cause here by sending us money. In fact, during the Ram Mandir movement, they were very generous. Then that masjid was demolished, which was something very good. Shri Ramesh Shah was in the forefront of rejoicing after the masjid was demolished. Now his daughter has been anointed and it is good for Hindus the world over.

There was hope among Hindutva circles in India that Shah's White House appointment would finally secure a visa for Narendra Modi to enter the United States.

It's no surprise that some of Shah's antecedents would be happy in John Podesta's Center for American Progress. Podesta played a role in the mysterious Democracy Alliance, the group of high rollers around the Democratic Party who were frustrated with the Clinton theory of triangulation and wanted a more robust liberalism to command their party (it was for a time presided over by Rob McKay, the Taco Bell heir who gave some of his millions to finance the San Francisco living wage battle). The Democracy Alliance came together to bridge the gap between the two arguments that tore at the Democratic Party in the Bush years. The principled argument ran between those who pushed a more liberal strategy and those who wanted to take Clintonian pragmatism to its limit. The organizational argument took place between those who felt that the Democratic Party should compete in all fifty states (Howard Dean) and those who wanted to maintain the focus on the fourteen competitive states (Rahm Emanuel). This was a bitter battle. Podesta's calmness usefully held these two sections together. His CAP, in fact, not only became a neutral ground for these two sections of the Democratic Party, but it also had ambitions to link the party to the various progressive movements that lay on its outer rim and beyond.

Many of the center's ideas, however, strayed far from progressivism, keener to be bold against its base (such as teacher's unions) than against the world of finance. A study by CAP complained about teacher absence in the public schools (ten days a year), something that disproportionately impacted students in low-income neighborhoods. But not a word about the ruin of social welfare by the Clinton White House that resulted in the lack of institutions to shore up parents, teachers, and students in these neighborhoods. For our intrepid liberals it is far easier to utilize their calculus of triangulation to blame the teachers.

On foreign policy, the champions of humanitarian interventionism based at CAP remained confident, regardless of the failures in Afghanistan and Iraq. These are blamed on Bush's incompetence rather than on the exhaustion of U.S. imperialism. To revive their interventionist fantasies, CAP liberals use Darfur. It stiffens the spine. John Prendergast held the reins here, running ENOUGH, a CAP project. He is committed to the merits of doing something in Darfur but has little sense of the role that Darfur plays within the United States in keeping the terminally ill concept of humanitarian interventionism alive (Prendergast's line is skewered by Mahmood Mamdani in his sober-minded *Survivors and Saviors*). Right after Obama's election, Predergast co-wrote a letter asking the president-elect to "lead a concerted international peace surge for Sudan." This letter went out just as violence increased in the Great Lakes region of Africa (ground zero for the Cell Phone Wars of our day; the region is the source of coltan, an essential element in cell phones) and as Israel's armies once more struck the civilian populations of Gaza. Not a word from CAP on this. Nor on the Gujarat violence, nor the killing of the Christians by the Hindu Right. No humanitarian interventionism when it affects U.S. imperial interests. This is why Shah's own far Right commitments in India are not contradictory to those of CAP liberals; many of them have similar commitments to the far Right in Israel or in other parts of the world.

When asked to name his favorite books, Obama mentioned that one of them is Gandhi's *The Story of My Experiments with Truth*. I encourage him to go back to his edition (mine is Beacon Press, 1957) and turn to page 155. There he will find a simple sentence: "It has always been a mystery to me how men can feel themselves honored by the humiliation of their fellow-beings." The Hindu Right thrives on the humiliation of Indian Muslims, Christians, and oppressed castes, and it derives its social power from those who are survivors of the failed experiment in globalization. Those millions, like myself, who felt a joy in snubbing the Bush dynamic and the entire history of social exclusion in the United States demanded that our hopes be held to a higher standard. Not to the howling dogs, but to the doves.

SIGNALS OF ANOTHER FUTURE

On March 6, 2008, months before Obama's election, a hundred workers from a Pascagoula, Louisiana, shipyard walked off the job. These skilled workers came to the United States from India (mainly Kerala) to work for Signal International, an oil services firm that overhauls and repairs oil rigs.

Hurricane Katrina devastated the Gulf Coast, which meant that it also wreaked havoc in the oil facilities that dot the coastline from Florida to Texas. A year after the hurricane, Rita J. King authored a devastating report, *Big, Easy Money*, on the reconstruction efforts in Louisiana: "The devastation of the Gulf Coast is tragic enough, but the scope of the corporate greed that followed, facilitated by government incompetence and complicity, is downright criminal. Well-connected corporations are growing rich off of no-bid contracts while the subcontractors, the people who actually perform the work, often do so for peanuts, if they get paid at all." To rebuild the coastline, including the city of New Orleans, firms and municipalities (via subcontractors) turned to the cheapest possible workforce: either undocumented workers or workers who came to the United States on "guest worker" (H2B temporary worker) programs. Victoria Cintra of the Mississippi Immigrant Rights Alliance told King that the reconstruction workers were largely comprised of undocumented migrants from Mexico and Central America who earned a meager amount and lived in rickety trailers "not fit for rats." Rosana Cruz, the Gulf Coast field coordinator for the National Immigration Law Center, concurred with this description: "The level of assault against workers feels like war. There's vulnerability in each successive layer of subcontracting."

Signal, therefore, did not directly seek out these workers. They turned to an Indian jobber, Dewan Consultants, who advertised for these jobs and recruited and assembled the workers who then came to the United States. The workers were promised that they would be put on the road to a green card (or permanent residency), and that their working conditions would be reasonable. In 2006, about five hundred skilled metalworkers came to Louisiana after paying $20,000 to Signal's recruiters. This, of course, meant that the workers' families had to go into considerable debt, some even by selling their family land or homes. The family debt was an anchor that prevented the workers from leaving their jobs at Signal. They needed to make the money back. If they left the Signal jobs, they would be sent back to India. In other words, their right to express their opinions was circumscribed by a system that virtually indentured them to the company.

The Indian workers began to complain that they had been lied to regarding their green cards. They also felt that the housing they received was miserable ("24 narrow bunk beds, connected by plywood walkways," according to *Forbes*). Signal did not want to tolerate these "chronic whiners," as its chief operating officer Ronald Schnoor later said in a deposition to the Federal District Court in New Orleans. The firm approached Immigration and Customs Enforcement (ICE) officials to get some "guidance" on how to deal with the restive workers. Schnoor was very clear about what the ICE officials said: "Don't give them any advance notice. Take them out of the line on the way to work; get their personal belongings; get them in a van, and get their tickets, and get them to the airport, and send them back to India."

On March 9, 2007, Signal did as it was told. One worker, Sabulal Vijayan, who had been particularly angry about the work conditions and the visa lies, said he needed to go to the toilet, went into a trailer, and slit his wrists: "I slit my wrists to kill myself. There was no option for me." Protests outside the camp gates and Vijayan's suicide attempt stalled Signal's attempt to follow the ICE plan. "It was theatrics, a bunch of nonsense," Signal's chief executive Richard Marler told *Forbes*. "We want this program to work out. We need the labor." Signal denies any culpability, and so did the Indian jobber, Dewan Consultants. The Mumbai-based firm told the *Hindustan Times*, "If they found the living conditions unfit, they should have come back then, instead of making a hue and cry now."

Dewan is off the job. It was replaced by S. Mansur & Company, which the *Times of India* suggested might be a front for Dewan itself.

Signal's story is not novel to New Orleans and Louisiana. In recent years, similar stories have been brought to the fore by the New Orleans Workers' Center for Racial Justice (NOWCRJ), which itself was formed in 2005 by local activists who were alarmed by the miserable state of labor relations in the state during post-Katrina reconstruction. Shortly after the hurricane, the federal government suspended the laws that forced employers in disaster areas to pay workers the prevailing wage rates. In addition, the contracts for the reconstruction went to firms that had no intention of hiring the displaced population of the city.

In the aftermath of Hurricane Katrina, all signs indicated that the property owners and the political class wanted to take advantage of the moment to cleanse the city of its African American poor and to make the city a park for tourism and commerce. Stuck in Houston or in federal disaster relief trailers, working-class African Americans were not able to return to the city. The few choices for these displaced workers narrowed even more when the contractors refused to hire them. In a valuable study published in 2006, NOWCRJ assembled stories of African American workers who had been shut out from the reconstruction in *And Injustice for All: Workers' Lives in the Reconstruction of New Orleans*. Marlon Tibbs, a construction worker, told NOWCRJ, "I was trying to find work. They looked over the people who were born and raised here." Drawing from such interviews, NOWCRJ concluded, "Blacks have been and are being excluded from employment in redevelopment jobs, particularly in the construction industry."

Instead of hiring local residents and helping them get back on their feet, the construction firms and local industries turned to migrant workers, mainly from Mexico and Latin America, but also from Asia. There are an estimated hundred thousand such workers in the Gulf region, working in the construction trades and in places such as various ports along the Gulf Coast. The firms that hired these immigrants, many without legal documents, used their vulnerable status to pay them less than minimum wage and treat them appallingly. One study found that "a quarter of the workers rebuilding the city were immigrants lacking papers, almost all of them Hispanic, making far less money than legal workers." Workers at a Halliburton job site said that their subcontractors would threaten them with deportation as a way to make them live in constant fear. Journalist Naomi Klein recounts, "Most workers fled to avoid arrest; after all, they could end up in one of the new immigration prisons that Halliburton/KBR had been contracted to build for the federal government." To combat the fear of deportation, NOWCRJ and its allies started a Right to Remain campaign. It fought to allow those who came to rebuild the city the right to build a life in it as well.

The workers at Signal were hired in India or in the Persian Gulf, many of them veterans of the guest worker networks. Just as skilled Indian workers have begun to protest the bad work conditions in Dubai, so too are they now standing up for their rights in the United States. The striking workers carried signs that read "Dignity" and "I Am a Man," phrases used by black workers during the strike wave of the late 1960s. The displaced

African American workers gave their support to these Indian workers, both groups of whom have been carefully organized by NOWCRJ into the Alliance of Guest Workers for Dignity. The linkage between the displaced black workers and the exploited Indian workers is a rebuke to the divide-and-conquer strategy of the political class. This view is rejected by the vibrant alliance envisaged by NOWCRJ.

NOWCRJ and the five hundred workers have sued Signal. NOWCRJ's Saket Soni said, "The U.S. State Department calls it a 'repulsive crime' when recruiters and employers in other parts of the world bind guest workers with crushing debts and threats of deportation. This is precisely what is happening on the Gulf Coast." Vijayan put it plainly, "We are saying that this is modern-day slavery." The *New York Times*'s Julia Preston wrote a pointed story on the collusion between Signal and ICE, and highlighted a lawsuit brought by the U.S. government's Equal Employment Opportunity Commission ("Suit Points to Guest Worker Program Flaws," February 2, 2010), on which basis the newspaper ran a sharp editorial on this "sad tale of human trafficking" ("A Bitter Guest Worker Story," February 4, 2010). At no time did Governor Bobby Jindal make a stand for these workers. At no point, as well, was it even reasonable to assume that the state would do right by the workers. They became a pawn in someone else's game.

The workers felt that Jindal might be sympathetic to them. The Indian community in the state felt that he would make some special statement when two Indian graduate students (Chandrasekhar Reddy Komma and Kiran Kumar Allam) were killed at Louisiana State University in December 2007. Governor-elect Jindal, whose transition headquarters were also on the LSU campus, remained silent. So did the entire political class. They remain trapped by a discussion that does not seem to listen to the black displaced workers and the striking Indian workers, both of whom point their hard hats at the corporations and not at each other. There was no compulsion of ethnicity to support them. The lead organizer at NOWCRJ is Saket Soni, himself a migrant from India, whose family hails from Punjab.

I began this chapter with Raj Rajaratnam's case. The U.S. Attorney who pursued him is Preet Bharara, like Jindal and Haley from Punjab, born in Ferozepur to a Hindu mother and a Sikh father. He is not disposed to those in power or those who want to add an extra zero to their cache of millions.

All these Punjabis, on all sides of the fence.

6

The Honeycomb Comes Apart

If beings in heaven are gratified by our offering the *sraddha*
here, then why not give the food down below to those who are
standing on the housetop?

— *Sarva-darsana-samgraha*

I was raised in a mixed family. My parents' families came to
Bengal from Punjab and from Burma. One side leans toward
Hinduism; the other to Sikhism. The city, the metro, provided
its own cultural mooring, and in secular India, I found my-
self interested in all religions and deeply schooled in none.
Id meant fellowship with my Muslim neighbors and friends;
a Navjot meant a crash course in Parsi life; Nanak's birthday
meant a visit to Gurudwara Sant Kutiya in the center of town;
Christmas, which is Bara Din in Calcutta, meant a brightly lit
Park Street and a visit to St. Paul's Cathedral; and Diwali and
Holi represented the high points of our street festival culture.
Religion was colorful and friendly. It didn't represent either the
harshest of personal morality nor the resentments or distrust of
others.

I learned a few prayers and songs, but this learning was not

systematic. Some of my friends were better schooled than I
in their various traditions. Our diversity was not simply across
religion but also a diversity of the density of our engagement
with religion: agnostics or religious illiterates were as welcome
as those who were committed to their faith. The festival that I
most liked was Saraswati Puja, the day when we wore yellow
and put all our schoolbooks at the feet of the goddess. The
respite from study was welcome.

My morality came from elsewhere than religion, from recognition of the pain in the world. Religious teachers whom I
encountered sometimes talked about this suffering, but they
didn't seem to have more than charity to offer to those who suffered. It struck me that while religious festivals were beautiful,
religions themselves were not adequate as a solution to modern crises. But religion, as I came to understand while reading
Gandhi many years later, can play a role in the cleansing of
public morality. In 1940, Gandhi wrote, "I still hold the view
that I cannot conceive politics as divorced from religion. Indeed, religion should pervade every one of our actions. Here
religion does not mean sectarianism. It means a belief in or-
dered moral government of the universe. It is not less real because it is unseen. This religion transcends Hinduism, Islam,
Christianity, etc. It does not supersede them. It harmonizes
them and gives them reality" (*Harijan*, February 10, 1940). In
other words, politics should not be simply about power struggles; it must be suffused with moral concerns. It is not enough
to win; one must strive to create what Gandhi called Truth in
the world. Gandhi would often forget his own lessons, and con-
fuse Truth with the transcendental religious traditions. This
is the reason he alienated those who had other faiths or none

at all. They suspected that beneath the language of interfaith concourse lay a broad appreciation of a reconstructed Hinduism. Gandhi did not explicitly walk away from the tradition of Hindu revivalism, which was the vehicle for the transfusion of the ideology of the Hindu landlords into both the Congress Party and Indian society. This was his limitation.

To strive for Truth does not mean that we, as humans, can be sure that what we believe in or what we aspire to is some transcendental truth. Gandhi's autobiography was not called *I've Found Truth*, but *The Story of My Experiments with Truth*. The use of the word "experiments" is revealing, since it refers to a scientific tradition that privileges verifiable testing. (This is also the case with the Gujarati word "prayago," which is in the original 1927 title, *Satya-na Prayago athva Atmakatha*; Professor Babu Suthar links "prayoga," the singular of "prayago," to the ayurvedic and yogic sense of treatment and practice. An ayurvedic doctor must ask the patient to "prayoga" a medicine, which would imply trying it out to see if it works.) Religious traditions are resources to guide us, as social individuals, through the difficulties and opportunities of our lives. They are not dogmas to tear people apart from each other. In a powerful essay against compulsory widow segregation, Gandhi wrote, "It is good to swim in the waters of tradition, but to sink in them is suicide" (*Navajivan*, June 28, 1925). Let tradition be a studied resource, not a set of inflexible, unchanging rules.

RESURRECTION

Raised in a circle of privilege in Calcutta, I was not prepared to recognize the world's trials. Looking out of my window at the poverty and squalor, I could see weakness and danger—not the flotsam of a system that had *purposely* treated human beings like garbage. The morality that my liberal surroundings taught me was constrained by a general feeling of humanism (feel bad for the condition of humanity at large) but not to act for the specific conditions of those who lived around us. For the latter, the real, living humans, there was only charity. We had little else to offer. The worst among us even begrudged the charity, arguing that it took away incentive from the impoverished and made them unwilling to work. I didn't come from that kind of world, but yet my world, the best of the privileged, could only march us down to hand out food to the poor once a year or collect our old clothes and take them down to the local *basti*, where we would make eye contact with our peers as they took our clothes for their bodies. It was miserable, but it was, at least, something.

In my early teens I encountered two authors who helped me move forward. Reading Premchand's short stories gave me my first entry point into the emotional world of the working class and the peasantry. To be sure, his stories are set in the country-side and I lived in the city. And so his stories said little about the post-1947 condition of urban class conflict, the seething frenzy of resentment and mutual distrust that is controlled by high walls and *darwans* and mediated by domestic servants who must traverse the class lines. But nonetheless, from Prem-chand I learned a little of what it meant to live on the other side of the tracks, to forge a consciousness that was at once aware of deprivation but yet which sought the comforts of love and leisure. There is *Kafan* and *Idgah*, but also *Jyoti* and *Gulli Danda*. The joys, the sorrows, the errors, the humanity, and, centrally, the outrageous power bloc that wields its weapons against those who are just trying to get by. I was enraptured by the social condition of lives that otherwise simply went by me.

One day, at a Soviet bookstall, I found myself drawn to a book that I knew nothing about. The cover was rather foreboding: it was a dark painting, with a large man whose white beard gave contrast to his black cloak. He glared at me. I bought the book. It was Leo Tolstoy's *Resurrection* (1899). I remember being dragged into the story, unable to let go. It told the tale of Prince Nekhlyudov, a rich and young nobleman who has sex with Maslova, his aunt's servant. She is ruined by the events that follow, most of them spurred on by the night with Nekhlyudov. The prince is distraught and tries his best to make amends. Nekhlyudov regenerates his life, giving everything up to be beside a haggard and beaten Maslova as she makes her way to the prison camps of Siberia. He cannot defeat the system, cannot free her. Even his exulted status is insufficient. That, to me, was the truly remarkable part of the novel—the failure of an elite individual to exert his nascent liberalism on behalf of an individual whose life he had participated in ruining. Nekhlyudov holds the stage: it is his act that sets the plot in motion, it is his personal march through the institutions to save Maslova that concerns the reader, and it is his sacrifice that moves us. Maslova and her class provide the backdrop. We are moved by them, chastised by them, but not able to see them as agents of change. Theirs is a sorrowful march, a pageant of suffering that is to give us, the bourgeois readers, pause. This is the limit of liberalism.

Many years later, when I was reading Lenin's writings, I came upon his 1908 critique "Leo Tolstoy as the Mirror of the

Russian Revolution." Lenin was never the best literary critic, largely because he was impatient with sentiment, with nuance. He wanted characters like Maslova to throw their fists in the air, to break down the walls of privilege. But writers like Tolstoy were not given to letting their creations disrupt the quiet rooms where they worked. Lenin searched for Maslova, to organize her against Nekhlyudov, not to allow the prince his resurrection from his pain. "Tolstoy reflected the pent-up hatred, the ripened striving for a better lot, the desire to get rid of the past," Lenin wrote, "and also the immature dreaming, the political inexperience, the revolutionary flabbiness." Lenin laid out the contradictions in Tolstoy, who, on the one hand, provides "merciless criticism of capitalist exploitation, exposure of government outrages, the farcical courts and the state administration, and unmasking of the profound contradictions between the growth of wealth and achievements of civilization and the growth of poverty, degradation and misery among the working masses," and who, on the other hand, hastily takes refuge in Christian pacifism and submission. Maslova is quiet but determined. She tells us, with her rejection of Nekhlyudov, that she is not waiting to be rescued by her prince on a white horse. But she is also not invested in a systemwide change. There are no organizers, no Narodniks, nobody who might put the stubborn determination of the millions of Maslovas into motion. Tolstoy didn't have that in him.

What Tolstoy and Premchand gave me was a tangible experience in the limit of liberalism. Good feelings of charity are often more for the bourgeois than for the deprived: it makes us feel good to give, doing nothing as it were to change the system of deprivation. For that there are other books, other worlds.

But before getting there it was essential to break the faith in the capacity for change within such an immutable system, to walk away from an unprincipled peace toward something better. Perhaps that is the true message of *Resurrection*, that the labors of Nekhlyudov were not capable of moving the old granite block of power. More is needed.

When I read Gandhi, as every Indian child does at some point, I experienced the same kind of claustrophobia as I did when I read Tolstoy. It is no coincidence that the Indian was influenced by the Russian (Gandhi read Tolstoy's *The Kingdom of God Is Within You*, 1894, and corresponded with him in 1910; Tolstoy's "Letter to a Hindu" was written in 1908 to Taraknath Das and implored Indians to use love as the means to fight the British in India. Gandhi translated it into Gujarati). Neither had room for the initiative and the intellect of the masses, nor for the structural deprivations that had to be recast for a new world to be reborn. Imperialism had to be fought on the political terrain, for both Gandhi and Tolstoy, but it would only be defeated spiritually. This was something that I did not accept.

THE GITA

Fifteen years ago, I was teaching South Asian history in central New York. A few young students invited me to their Gita reading group. I was delighted to join them, not because I was an expert in the Gita, but because it pleased me to see South Asian Americans take an interest in the history and traditions of the subcontinent. The students dutifully read their section for the evening and proceeded to have a discussion about it.

They had little guidance apart from the text, and they valiantly drew from the analytical skills they learned in their classes to make sense of the Gita. For them, religion was not an "experiment with truth," but because of the context, it was the Truth that had to be unmasked by their close, devoted reading. I felt myself sinking into it.

The Gita is a remarkable book, precisely because of its history (it was composed long after the Mahabharata, written in the classical Sanskrit of the Gupta era and interpolated into the long epic much later). Frustrated with the hierarchy promoted by Brahmans through the Vedic traditions, scores of people turned to Sramanic traditions (most familiarly, Buddhism). The Gita is a sublime response to the power of Buddhism with concepts such as karma drawn from it. The genius of the text is that it takes concepts and ideas from these popular traditions and brings them into line with some of the central principles of Brahmanism (*varna*, mainly). The Gita is awash with contradictions: it preaches *ahimsa*, and yet is set in a battlefield, where Krishna must convince Arjun to go into the fight; it validates the importance of caste hierarchy, and yet shines a light on the equality of all before the awesome might of divinity. The contradictory nature of the text allows every reader to find something beneficial in it. It works as a mirror to our reality.

Then there is *bhakti*, one of the foundation stones of modern Hinduism. It is the Gita's central concept. Personal devotion (bhakti) drew from the oppressed peoples of the subcontinent the ability to challenge those who stood between them and divinity (the Brahmans, for instance) and those who stood between them and a peaceful life (kings, for instance). The concept of bhakti was the central idea for a series of important spiritual and social rebellions, led by such people as Andal, Kabir, Mirabai, Tukaram, and, above all, Jnanesvar. Jnanesvar, the thirteenth-century Marathi poet, wrote an extended commentary on the Gita in which he not only went after the powerful but also bemoaned the great harm done to the people for whom religion had become a crutch rather than an engine. "The peasant farmer sets up cult after cult, according to convenience," he wrote. "He follows the preacher who seems most impressive at the moment, learns his mystic formula. Harsh to the living, he relies upon stones and images; but even then never lives true to any one of them." Jnanesvar's powerful critique was not met with an equally powerful movement to overthrow the foundation of the social order of his time. As the historian D.D. Kosambi wrote, "Though an adept in *yoga* as a path towards physical immortality and mystical perfection, there was nothing left for [Jnanesvar] except suicide." The ideas were glorious, but there was no institutional platform to realize them.

NOXIOUS HINDUTVA

All this is lost if one reads the Gita as settled Truth rather than an experiment in truth. When Gandhi claimed to base his ahimsa philosophy on the Gita, he faced opposition. "My claim to Hinduism has been rejected by some," he wrote in *Young India* (May 29, 1924),

> because I believe [in] and advocate non-violence in its extreme form. They say that I am a Christian in disguise. I have been even seriously told that I am distorting the

meaning of the Gita when I ascribe to that great poem
the teaching of unadulterated non-violence. Some of my
Hindu friends tell me that killing is a duty enjoined by
the Gita under certain circumstances. A very learned
Shashtri only the other day scornfully rejected my interpretation of the Gita and said that there was no warrant
for the opinion held by some commentators that the Gita
represented the eternal duel between forces of evil and
good, and inculcated the duty of eradicating evil within
us without hesitation, without tenderness. . . . My religion is a matter solely between my Maker and myself.
If I am a Hindu, I cannot cease to be one even though I
may be disowned by the whole of the Hindu population.

Those who criticized Gandhi for his "misuse" of Hinduism
came from the organizations of the Right. The Hindu Mahas-
abha (1915) and the Rashtriya Swayamsevak Sangh (1925)
provided this Right with an institutional nucleus to sharpen
the assault on both Indian society and on the Indian freedom
movement (whose undisputed leader at this time was Gandhi).
The leadership of this Right considered Gandhi a "traitor" to
the "Hindu people," and it was their cadre that murdered him
in 1948. The RSS, the spearhead of the new "Hindu nationalism," eschewed the mass freedom struggle that emerged in
the 1920s, sharpened in the 1930s, and eventually defeated the
British Raj in the 1940s. In 1928, the RSS inaugurated its Officer Training Camp to train its own storm troopers—not to do
battle with the powerful British and its institutions but with the
relatively powerless Muslim masses. The *swayamsevak*, or volunteer, took an oath, "offering himself entirely—body, mind,

and wealth—for the preservation and progress of the Hindu Nation." The complexity of India—its diverse heritages and its fluid cultural resources—was anathema to the RSS and its doctrine of Hindutva.

The influence of Italian fascism and German Nazism pervaded the RSS, as clarified in the 1939 book by M.S. Golwalkar: "Germany has shown how well nigh impossible it is for Races and cultures, having differences going to the root, to be assimilated into one united whole, a good lesson for us in Hindustan to learn and profit by." For Golwalkar, the role of the "Jew" within India was to be played by the "Muslim" (it should be said that his 1939 book was reprinted in 1944 and in 1947, after the Holocaust was know to all, and yet there was no revision of this section). No wonder Nobel Prize winner Amartya Sen considered the ideology of the RSS to be "communal fascism." The RSS remained a marginal element in Indian political life, having played no role in the freedom struggle and having a noxious view of the complexity of Indian social life that appealed only to a few among the dominant castes who felt left out of the new Indian republic.

INDIAN HONEYCOMB

That complexity is something that Gandhi and others well understood. In 1992, the Anthropological Society of India published the first of an ongoing series of monographs with the omnibus title *The People of India*. In this volume, the late K.S. Singh laid out the basic findings of this immense study of the Indian people. There are, he wrote, 4,635 identifiable communities in India, "diverse in biological traits, dress, language,

forms of worship, occupation, food habits, and kinship patterns. It is all these communities who in their essential ways of
life express our national popular life." Strikingly, the scholars
working under Singh's direction discovered the immense over-
lap across religious lines. They identified 775 traits that related
to ecology, settlement, identity, food habits, marriage patterns,
social customs, social organization, economy, and occupation.
What they found was that Hindus share 96.77 percent traits
with Muslims, 91.19 percent with Buddhists, 88.99 percent
with Sikhs, 77.46 percent with Jains (Muslims, in turn, share
91.18 percent with Buddhists and 89.95 percent with Sikhs).
Singh pointed out that because of this, Indian society was like a
honeycomb, where each community is in constant and meaningful interaction with every other community. The boundar-
ies between communities are more a fact of self-definition than
of cultural distinction. This Gandhi knew implicitly. Unity was
a fact of life, not a conceit of secular theory.

When I went to Punjab in the early 1990s to do my dis-
sertation research, I was startled to find communities that
considered themselves on the fence about their religious
identification. Three in particular (that make their way into
Singh's study) stood out: the Mirasi, Sonar, and Rajputs, who
claimed to be both Hindus and Muslims. The group I had
gone to study, the Balmikis, had a wonderfully rich religious
history, where they crafted their own spiritual tradition around
the preceptor Bala Shah Nuri and Lalbeg. Bala Shah's poems
attacked both the Brahmans and the mullahs for their perpetu-
ation of untouchability and their refusal to stand for justice.
Ram te Rahim kian chhap chhap jana (the followers of Ram
and Rahim will hide themselves in fear), *sava neze te din avega,*

hade dosakh pana (and when the sun sets, Bala will send them to hell). This evokes the kind of language of that other great Punjabi poet, Bulle Shah, who sang, *Musalman sarne to dared hindu dared gor, dove ese vich mard eho duha di khor* (Muslims fear the flame, Hindus the tomb; both die in this fright, such is their hatred).

Hindutva, or the ideology and movement of Hindu chauvinism, attempts to do to this richness what agribusinesses do to biodiversity. They want to reduce the multiplicity and plurality of cultural forms into the one that they are then able to control: a deracinated "Hindu," like a genetically modified form of rice or barley. The joy of religious life, of social life, is reduced into a mass-produced form of worship, cultivated out of hatred for other religions rather than fellowship for humanity. With the RSS and its *parivar* (family), we are no longer in the land of religion. We are now in the land of power and politics, hate and resentment.

Until the 1980s, the RSS remained on the margins of Indian politics. Rejected at the ballot, the movement emerged only through assassination and intimidation, through riots and mayhem, by which it sought to define the political and social space. In the 1980s, conditions changed as the Congress Party abandoned its soft socialism/soft secularism for neoliberal globalization and the politicization of religion (first by patronizing Sikh separatists). The RSS family won over the Congress Party's "Hindu vote bank" through an aggressive campaign against *dalits* (over the Mandal Commission's attempt to deepen reservations), against Muslims (over the Meenakshipuram conversions and the controversy over the mosque at Ayodhya), and against the Left (by deeming its ideology to be "foreign").

Flamboyant campaigns designed to make the most of the television media and its harsh rhetoric against minorities attracted the dispossessed, who now joined with disgruntled dominant castes to bring the BJP to power.

In the 1980s, it was not simply Hindutva that found its feet. The collapse of the secular experiment let loose the growth of political Islam and Sikhism as well as neoliberal consumerism. The latter had no intention of trying to create a social order based on just principles, and the former wished (like their Hindutva friends) to found religious orders of justice that often meant going to battle with other religious orders. These were all toxic experiments, far removed from the secular one that they attempted to displace and supersede. The alienation was such that in California gurudwaras of the 1990s it had become uncomfortable for Hindus to gain entry, as they had in such Sikh houses of worship for centuries. The guardians of this purity were often Sikh men with black turbans to signal their alienation. The growth of Islamophobia and the emergence of Hindutva enveloped desi Muslims in their own cocoon of fear and anger, with mosques a mirror of the temples and spaces for convivial fellowship few and far between.

The Indian honeycomb began to break up in this period.

YANKEE HINDUTVA

In *The Karma of Brown Folk*, I used the term "Yankee Hindutva" to describe the way Hindu chauvinism came into the United States. Eager to branch out to the diaspora, the RSS and its subsidiaries took advantage of multiculturalism to build their foothold here. Not for the American audience did they use an unadulterated anti-Muslim rhetoric (that would come only in some "safe" spaces, and more aggressively, after 9/11). Initially, the RSS organizations, particularly the Vishwa Hindu Parishad of America (VHPA) and its youth wing, the Hindu Students Council (HSC), promoted the idea that Hinduism is denigrated in the United States and that if other cultures are being celebrated, why not Hinduism too. This is an unimpeachable argument, but it came with some implementation problems. First, it assumed that "Hinduism" is a singular thing, not a clumsy name for a diversity of beliefs and affections that litter not only the subcontinent but also the South Asian diaspora (from Trinidad to Fiji). Second, because the VHPA and the HSC jumped in the game first, and because the most stringent are often best to claim to speak for a religion, the conservatives took control of this issue. There was no liberal critique of the denigration of Hinduism, and when liberals and radicals did dare to tread, the conservatives harshly shut the door to them as being inauthentic defenders of the culture. This was the tenor of the battle over the 2005–6 revisions of the California textbooks. We didn't like the old books either. But we didn't like the sanitized version of Indian history promoted by the conservatives. We wanted "India" to appear for what it is, a land of contradictions, not an unblemished "brand" that needs to be sold so that we can feel falsely proud.

In 1990, a group of committed activists of the hard Right formed the Hindu Students Council (HSC) in the woods of New Jersey. Their public pronouncement was along the grain of liberal multiculturalism—that they wanted to assist Hindu students who struggle with the "loss and isolation" due to their "upbringing in a dual culture [as] Hindu and Judeo-Christian.

. . . We try to reconcile our own sorrows and imperfections as human beings in a variety of self-defeating ways. And we usually go through this confused internal struggle alone. It was precisely to assist you with [these] spiritual, emotional, and identity needs that HSC was born." Given the strictures of liberal multiculturalism, everyone, including college administrators, stood by and applauded. But the HSC was never simply about the identity struggles of those whom it called Hindu Americans. It was also the youthful fingers of the long arm of Hindutva supremacy in India. By its own account, the HSC is a "project of the Vishwa Hindu Parishad of America," the far Right "cultural wing" of the hard Right Sangh Parivar (Family of the Faithful). When activists of the Right destroyed a five-hundred-year-old mosque in 1992, the VHP egged them on, the VHPA cheered, and so did the leaders of the HSC. For them, concern over the identity struggles of young Indian Americans could easily be reconciled with their anti-Muslim politics. Multiculturalism in the United States provided cover for the cruel, cultural chauvinism in India.

Young South Asian Americans came to the HSC not always for its politics but for its space for shelter and struggle against anti-Indian racism. Falguni Trivedi, who participated in the HSC in 1997, tells the story poignantly: "When I was twelve years old, American kids would gang up on me at the bus stop, yelling 'Gandhi Dot' and ask, 'Why do you people in India worship cows and drink cow urine?' It is pretty tough for young Hindus stuck between two cultures." When Trivedi went to her parents, they, like many first-generation migrants, offered her the ostrich strategy. "Adjust" to the verbal abuse, they said. Trivedi, however, wanted her parents to offer clear answers to

the questions posed by the racist youth, such as answers about
the cow. The parents didn't have ready answers. "Parents don't
know," said Dheeraj Singhal, now a lawyer in Ohio. "They're
lost. They don't know where to look. Kids are really desperate
to know who they are, the meaning of their customs. This giant
void of ignorance facing them is a great issue." It is here that
the HSC and other such organizations (including the noncom-
munal South Asian Student Associations on various college
campuses) come in. But the HSC is actually unable or ill-fitted
to deal with U.S. racism. It tells the youth that they come from
an ancient heritage and that they should be proud of it, but the
HSC makes no attempt to undermine the structures of racism
that produce this sort of off-the-cuff racist remark. To promote
Indians as the "model minority" who have a great and ancient
culture, and not combat the racism that devastates the world of
color and pits people of color against each other, is inadequate.
It simply lifts up one minority, us, and says that we shouldn't
take this nonsense because we are culturally great.

Groups like the HSC and the VHPA are less concerned
with the broad problem of racism and of Indian American life
than they are with pushing the Hindutva agenda in the United
States and Canada. Here are two examples.

Air-Conditioned Sadhus

By the late 1990s, Hindu temples could be found in most
of the areas where Indian Americans lived (or where American Hindus did, as in Hawaii). The Prathishtapanas for the
Middletown, Connecticut, Satyanarayan temple near where
I live took place in 1999 (although families in the area had

worshipped in their basements since the early 1980s). These temples are a resource for Hinduism, with ceremonies and festivals, "Sunday Schools" and devotional sessions. The VHPA has other ideas for the temples. In 1998, at a VHPA Dharam Sansad, the conclave decided that all temples and cultural organizations "should associate, endorse and/or affiliate with the VHPA to make the Hindu voice more effective." In 2000, the VHPA sent a hundred God-men from India on a Dharma Prachar Yatra "in a manner so that all of America is covered with Hindutva," as a VHPA activist put it. One of the tasks of the Yatra was for the sadhus to "clear the misconceptions about the VHP" and to assert "the VHP's point of view about issues like the Ayodhya movement and attacks on Christians." All talk of "interfaith dialogue" and of Hinduism as tolerance was out the window. These God-men went on tour not to offer solace, spiritual guidance, or to explain the travails of racism; they came out to plug the BJP, the VHP, and its campaigns against Muslims and Christians in India.

The God-men were treated like touring rock stars. Luckily I was teaching the Manavadharmasastra (the Laws of Manu) that semester: "A priest should always be alarmed by adulation as if it were poison and always desire scorn as if it were ambrosia" (II. 162). Our air-conditioned priests are far removed from even the barest humility asked of them by their calling.

Representing Hinduism

For decades, there has been an ongoing debate within the broad field of India Studies. Influenced by social historians who opened up the world of Indian popular culture and the

struggles of ordinary Indians, and by the intervention of Ed-
ward Said's *Orientalism* (1978), these scholars fought against
the racism and conservatism of the academy. Sanskrit studies,
for instance, treated India as an ancient resource with no lived
heritage of Hinduism; political scientists saw India in terms of
U.S. or British foreign policy, not in terms of what is in the best
interests of the Indian people. Graduate school in the 1980s
and early 1990s was a hive of conflict against what some of us
saw as a racist representation of the subcontinent.

In 2000, Rajiv Malhotra of the Infinity Foundation published a long essay against the tenor of Hinduism Studies in
the United States. As if he were a lonely pioneer, Malhotra
went hell-for-leather against the entire U.S. academy. Much
of what he said is correct (there is an insensitivity toward the
Hindu tradition, and a disregard for the real living Indians),
and it had been the basis for a long-standing debate around the
institutions. With his access to the Indian American media,
Malhotra (and the soon-to-be-formed Hindu American Foundation, or HAF) went after individual academics and then
the California sixth-grade textbooks. It was a lot of flash and
lightning: many of us liberals and radicals were already in the
thick of these fights, and much of our work had been fruitful.
But we were not invested simply in making India look good:
we wanted to ensure that the diversity of India's history and its
struggles would be represented in the curriculum and in the
research agendas. "The social science and history textbooks do
not give as generous a portrayal of Indian culture as they do of
Islamic, Jewish, Christian cultures," carped Malhotra. When
asked about the struggles of dalits and women in ancient India,
Suhag Shukla of the Hindu American Foundation grumbled,

"In terms of men and women, I think, first of all if you look at Christianity or Judaism or Islam, nowhere in the textbooks is there any discussion of women's rights. Then to pull it in for Hinduism, is a different treatment of Hinduism." All culture must have equal treatment, all contemporary representatives of that culture should be able to create their sense of self-worth based on this representation. Shukla has a point: no tradition is in the clear on these issues. The solution is not to brown-wash the textbooks on ancient Indian history but to write more honest books about the contradictions of all civilizations.

Malhotra's assault to get a politically correct interpretation accepted or nothing at all is the genteel version of the Shiv Sena and VHP activists in India who went after James Laine's book on Shivaji (by book burnings and physical assaults on his collaborators).

These issues are brought to the center by the VHPA, the HSC, and the HAF: all to blind us from other issues, such as racism in the United States, the Afghanistan and Iraq War, economic uncertainty and distress in India, increasing sexual assault and female infanticide in India, and the Gujarat pogrom. Yankee Hindutva is a set of blinders, not an optic to see the world clearly. It is as blind as political Islam, as blind as neoliberal consumerism. These are not adequate frameworks to make sense of a world that needs so much change.

WHAT WOULD YOU HAVE?

Over the past decade in the United States, the Hindutva Right and sections of the neoliberal elite moved to consolidate its agenda: closer ties between Indian American lobby groups and Israeli lobby groups, to sharpen the idea that the Indo-Pakistani problems can only be resolved in the Israeli fashion, through force; the creation of the Hindu American Foundation (whose main campaign in 2004–5 was the Diwali resolution, and who was an active leader of the California textbooks campaign); and an assault on scholars of India and Hinduism, led this time by the Infinity Foundation. But not a word was heard from any of these organizations on the farmers' suicides in Andhra Pradesh, on the deepening problem of unemployment across India, and on the cataclysmic child malnutrition rates across the country. These matters were not, apparently, of importance. Discussions about Brand India eclipsed the burgeoning social crises in India. Again, as Gandhi warned his fellows ninety years ago, "The test of orderliness in a country is not the number of millionaires it owns, but the absence of starvation among its masses" (Muir Central College Economics Society, Allahabad, December 22, 1916).

Equally, these organizations remained silent after 9/11 regarding the attacks on South Asians and Arabs and on the illegal detentions of hundreds of South Asians (the civil rights and activist groups, such as South Asian American Leaders of Tomorrow and Desis Rising Up and Moving, were in the lead here). Immigration reform, "Operation Meth Merchant" (against small Indian shopkeepers in Georgia), and other such issues were equally off the radar of the Hindu Lobby and the neoliberal consumerists. None of them had anything critical to say about the imperial assaults between the Hindu Kush and the Atlas Mountains, or the massive military spending in the United States that distorts the possibility of a social agenda for the people. On all these matters, silence.

The Hinduism that cares more for its reputation than for its relevance is no longer a living tradition. It has become some-*thing* that one reveres from a distance. To keep it alive, Hindu-ism requires an engagement with its history (which shows us how it evolves and changes) and with its core concepts (what we otherwise call philosophy). "Every formula of every religion has, in this age of reason, to submit to the acid test of reason and universal justice if it is to ask for universal assent," Gandhi wrote in 1925. "Error can claim no exemption even if it can be supported by the scriptures of the world" (*Young India*, Febru-ary 26, 1925). Submit all faith to experiments to see how they are able to assist one in the messy world we live in: to degrade faith into self-indulgence is to patronize those traditions. That's the nature of experimentation, a far better approach to faith traditions than empty reverence.

As the cliché goes, the subcontinent is the home to all reli-gions. Christianity and Judaism came to the region before they went to Europe. There are more Muslims in South Asia than elsewhere in the world. Buddhism was dispatched from the Gangetic plains for its adventures in the rest of Asia and now in the Atlantic countries. And of course, the people of the Vedas ended up on those plains, and out of their traditions, centuries later, came the Hinduism that is familiar today. But alongside and inside these religious traditions grew a sharp acknowledg-ment of the harshness of life that lay outside the delights prom-ised to humans if they obeyed their religious laws. It was from this realization that we got Kabir's *doha*:

Aasha jive jag marey, log marey mar jayee
Soyee sube dhan sanchte, so ubrey jey khayee.

Hope lives in a vanishing world, people die and die once
  more
Cease to hoard wealth. Gain your liberation by giving.

Religion in the subcontinent has, for a long time, had a
complex relationship with social hierarchy, sometimes its
bedfellow and other times its enemy. The classical saints of
the Sufi-Bhakti era mortified their bodies for the sake of the
masses; today's "saints" mortify the bodies of the masses for the
sake of the gain of the upwardly mobile. Our traditions seem
no longer able to fully carry forward their own self-professed
commitments to humanity. Attacks on religious minorities in
each of South Asia's countries are far too commonplace. One
does not see the established religious leaders take much interest in the grotesque suffering of the population, despite their
religious affiliations. It is a mark of shame that our religious
traditions, *all* our religious traditions, have paid so little interest
to the mounting suffering of the people, whether it's the farmers who resort to suicide or the migrants who must leave their
homes to work with little dignity in South Asia's burgeoning
cities. There is no Kabir today, no Bulleh Shah, no Buddha.
What we have, rather, is religion baring its fangs, not its heart.

The harshness of advanced capitalism has eroded the long
tradition of tolerance that has helped ordinary people fight off
the more stringent obligations of religious doctrine. People
have lived together for centuries, fought occasionally, but
mostly lived with the harmony of everyday life. It is this tradition that must form the basis for any institutional policies of
secularism. A secular state cannot sit well if it is not rooted in
the beliefs and habits of society. It cannot claim to be better

than the people, nor should it see itself as transplanted from elsewhere. South Asian secularism is a product of our history, inside the subcontinent and in its diaspora, one that has at its core the anticolonial and antihierarchical struggles that made us into modern states. Our civilization does not come from some abstract principles but from those very struggles in which ordinary people sacrificed much to ensure that the modern states held fast to the best of human morality (equality, justice, and so on). Secularism is the product of these struggles. Much that the anticolonial, antihierarchical struggles wanted has not, of course, come to pass. These struggles are ongoing. In the 1980s, as the various states in our region began to withdraw from the dirigisme that allowed the state to intervene in society, social groups given over to much less generous interpretations of religion emerged as if reborn. Chauvinisms of Hinduism, Islam, and Buddhism emerged in this era, pushing against the modest secularism of the modern states. Most of these new political blocs had no interest in the condition of starvation, keener to proclaim the need for national, if religious, pride. Die hungry, they seem to cry, but die with your religious standard in hand.

What we need is a path that takes us past the world's horrendous poverty into something that resembles equality. A roadblock right before us is the belief that religious chauvinism is a reasonable substitute for a good meal. It must be rejected. So too should we thrust away neoliberal consumerism, which assumes that the very process that creates inequality should be extended as a means to create freedom. Neither religious nor neoliberal messianism is worthwhile as a foundation for the future. Other hopes need the sunlight to grow.

The harsh edge of racism struck those who resembled terrorists right after 9/11. An important minority among us sought out safe harbors in religious chauvinism or in neoliberal consumerism. Others recognized the reality of the racism and joined together to push back against it. But what was universally ignored was the structural relationship between that racism and the imperialism that allows for aerial bombardment and extraordinary rendition, that links the archipelago of prisons that run along the spine of California's interior and the "black sites" for torture that run along the vein of North Africa and the Middle East and upward into Eastern Europe. Being active supporters of imperial adventures or of neoliberal degradation of subcontinental realities is as myopic as religious fanaticism. They too must be set aside.

The choice lies between giving over the traditions you love to the forces of hatred who might masquerade as the defenders of tradition (in religious terms) or as the promoters of progress (in economic terms), or to the force within you, and around you—a force of love and ecstasy, passion and pain—to transform the world.

What would you have?

INDEX